Into the Infinite

Opening the Door to the Unknown

by

Della Van Hise

~

A Quantum Shaman™ Book
www.quantumshaman.com

Into the Infinite
Opening the Door to the Unknown

Copyright © 2016
by Della Van Hise and Quantum Shaman™

ISBN: 978-1-942415-10-7
Published by Eye Scry Publications

2016 © All rights reserved. This book may not be reproduced wholly or in part without prior written permission from the publisher and author, except by a reviewer who may quote brief passages. Neither may any section of this book be reproduced, stored in a retrieval system, or transmitted in any form or by any means, electronic, mechanical, photocopying, recording or other, without prior written permission from the author, except as exempted by legitimate purchase through the author's website, Amazon.com or other authorized retailer.

To visit the author's website, please go to:
www.quantumshaman.com

Address all inquiries to:
info@quantumshaman.com

Quantum Shaman™ is a registered trademark

Piracy ruins lives!

This book is legally copyrighted © and MAY NOT be uploaded to any electronic storage center, website, or other such device/location. Period. End of argument. We are a small, independent company – if you upload this book to an illegal download site, you are robbing my family and my cats and dogs, who really do need to eat. You know better. Please don't do it!

For the ones I love...

Wendy
M
Styx

*...and all the allies and enigmas
I've encountered along the way*

Books in the Quantum Shaman™ Series

Quantum Shaman: Diary of a Nagual Woman
Scrawls On the Walls of the Soul
Questions Along the Way
Into the Infinite

All are available on Amazon, through your local retailer, or directly from our website at www.quantumshaman.com

Into the Infinite

INTRODUCTION

I once said to Wendy with regard to the subject of writing, "I don't want to be the one writing the books, I want to be the character on a grand and mysterious adventure!"

In ways too numerous to imagine, I have been granted that wish, even though I probably didn't believe it was possible at the time I first uttered those words sometime in the waning October of 1986 or thereabouts.

Many seekers of Knowledge have come to me over the years, lamenting the fact that they haven't yet stepped into that grand adventure. They find themselves stuck in the world of ordinary affairs, looking out through eyes of wonder and hope and finding only the sameness of work, family and - if they are lucky - an occasional dinner with friends.

I cannot tell you why I have been so fortunate to be showered with mysteries and mysticism, and why others - whom I might consider more deserving - have never encountered an ally or witnessed some inexplicable phenomenon, or even felt the hairs raise up on the back of their neck for no logical reason. My suspicion - and my true hope - is that it simply hasn't happened for them *yet*, and that as their own path progresses, they may find themselves face to face with an ally or a guardian or even their own mysterious and inexplicable double. For it is through our encounters with the unknown that we expand our horizons and push our limitations one increment further away.

In my own case, there may be something to the idea that being raised in a rural environment forces a child to develop their imagination, and that was certainly true for me. Growing up in central Florida as an only child guaranteed that certain social and cultural programming which is automatic in most families escaped me altogether. As a result, particularly in an age before computers and the internet, I was forced to create my own playmates entirely from my imagination and go on those grand adventures as a landing party of one.

Studies have been done on children who grow up in isolated environments as opposed to those who are brought up in more suburban climes, and there is certain evidence to suggest that isolated kids appear to be more intuitive and creative - though those same studies may be used to indicate that the isolated kids are more rebellious and may, in fact, have a few screws loose.

I'm not much for studies and what we are told we should believe because of them, but I can't deny that there *may* have been something in my upbringing - which was erratic and sporadic at best - that permitted me to escape almost entirely the enculturation process which programs children what is permissible to believe and what isn't.

At the age of 6, I went on one of my first grand adventures. I was off to the tropics to sail on the *Tiki* with her handsome captain, Adam Troy (played by Gardner McKay, who was an enigma and a mystery unto himself). I was there for several days, hanging out on what, to some, was a film set for the old television series, *Adventures In Paradise*, and to others (mainly myself) was the doorway to some Otherworld where I was all grown up and not just a toe-headed kid underfoot.

Of course, when our Sunday School teacher asked what we did on our summer vacation and I told the tale of my time with Captain Troy aboard the *Tiki*, my mother and Crazy Granny found it anything *but* amusing, and I was grounded for the rest of my life for telling such a fantastical tale, and - to *their* perceptions - such an outright lie.

Perception is reality - at least from a subjective perspective. To *my* perceptions, the events described not only happened, but are indelibly inked into my memory to this day. Perhaps some well-meaning shrink would say I hallucinated as a result of being bedridden with the measles at the time these events occurred. From *his* perception, that would also be true, but it was not *my* reality.

I mention these things only because I've found that we poor, frightened humans are so quick to dismiss anything that doesn't occur in ordinary awareness. To my mother's perception, as well as that of my Crazy Granny and the hypothetical shrink, if we didn't get on a plane and physically move our bodies from one location to another, we did not *really* go there. That is simply reality to their perceptions, and with a self-satisfied "Harrumph!" at the end of their proclamation.

And yet...

How often have we heard of altered states of consciousness wherein the traveler goes to far distant places and returns to his body to report locations and events not only accurately, but truly *as if* she were actually there? Of course, anyone on this journey of the heart full-well *knows* she was really there, because perception isn't limited to the five physical senses alone. Remote viewing has proven this, as well as experiments designed to test the veracity of astral travel and bilocation.

So often over the years, I've had seekers tell me their true tales of otherworldly encounters as if they are ashamed. Their head hangs low, they avert their eyes and speak in terms such as "Well, I *thought* I saw a ghost, but I know it must have been just a trick of the light." Or, "I was driving through the desert back in '66 and the trip should have taken 4 hours, but when I got to my destination, a full day had passed. I probably just lost track of time - who knows?" They then laugh nervously and brush their own words aside with a dismissive gesture.

I find such stories very disheartening - not for *what* these seekers are telling me, but for the fact that they have been ridiculed and shamed and - in some cases - reprogrammed to believe they should seek psychiatric help. This usually involves a bit of reprogramming at the level of anti-psychotic drug therapy - not because there is anything *wrong* with them, but because our culture will only allow for certain things to be admitted into the realms of "reality," automatically dismissing through fear anything that may not fit in a neat and tidy manner into their pre-existing ideas about what reality actually *is*.

The world is nothing like we've been taught to believe.

Some of us have experienced the truth behind that statement in a very up close and personal manner. We have been visited by spirits of the dead. Some have seen UFOs or even been "abducted by aliens," as the popular saying goes. Others have traveled extensively on the astral planes[1]. The tales of otherworldly encounters are endless - but it's important to remember that these events aren't really 'otherworldly' at all. As my own ineffable double is fond of saying, "There is only one world, divided infinitely by perception."

What society considers impossible today will be commonplace tomorrow. What science calls 'delusions' or even 'hallucinations' may be found to be visionary states or even travels outside the body. What shamans and mystics call their 'double' will be discovered to be an actual energetic projection which holds the potential to house our awareness beyond this physical life - not some quasi-religious angel or boogeyman, but a quantifiable construct of energy.

My own knowledge of the double comes from direct personal experience, and many of those experiences will form

---

[1] For anyone with a keen interest in astral travel, I recommend the books of Robert Monroe. *Far Journeys, Journeys Out of the Body,* and *Ultimate Journey.*

the foundation for this book. There is a relatively common belief here in the West that we are either born with a soul, or that we are the reincarnated essence of that soul moving between a plethora of lives. And while these belief systems may offer comfort to some, they cannot really compare with the personal power the seeker may gain when she comes into direct contact with the higher self.

    I have detailed many of my encounters with Orlando on the Quantum Shaman™ website[2] as well as in my first two books, Quantum Shaman (Diary of a Nagual Woman); and Scrawls On the Walls of the Soul. I would encourage the reader to look at these sources for some background information if possible - although it is my hope that the anecdotes presented in this book will stand on their own. Also, I would ask you to keep in mind that not all of these events are earth-shattering or life-altering in and of themselves. Instead, it is over a period of time that patterns begin to emerge, and the seeker begins to *see* that these are not random occurrences at all, but pieces of a much larger puzzle emerging from the shadows of the infinite.

    It is only when we *expand* our world and its perceptions that we empower ourselves to *change* the world and its perceptions. For as long as mystics and visionaries, and people who have experienced the ineffable are seen by the world as mad men and mad women, the world will remain a more narrow and limited milieu, never acknowledging its full potential.

    For those who have asked, "What do these experiences *mean*?"

    They mean we are human.
    We are still evolving.
    We are still growing.
    We are still learning.
    Instead of slamming the door on our potential, what

---

[2] http://www.quantumshaman.com/html/mirror.htm

might happen if we allowed it to open just a little, to see what might be on the other side? Maybe it will terrify us. Maybe it will amaze us or even amuse us.

Or just maybe... it will be the beginning of our own love affair with the unknown.

Della Van Hise - January 2016

EDITORIAL NOTE

The anecdotes presented in this book are offered entirely at random, in no specific order of linear time or relevance. Whenever possible, I have included the date, though for obvious reasons, some dates have been lost to the ages. Such is the fickle nature of time. For those who have not yet read Quantum Shaman (Diary of a Nagual Woman), it is recommended as a background companion piece to this one, as it is there (and on the Quantum Shaman™ website) that the story of Orlando appears in its entirety.

GLOSSARY

If you find words or phrases with which you are unfamiliar, may we recommend the Glossary located at the back of this book. The Glossary is also available online at http://www.quantumshaman.com/html/glossarytext.htm.

PREFACE

Magic is a Burden to Others
A Brief Overview of Why You Are Considered To Be A Pain-In-the-Ass

Sometimes we choose the magical world.
Other times it chooses us.
Most people don't really want magic in their lives.
What else can we call it? Supernatural phenomenon. Hauntings. Prophetic dreams. Visionary experiences. Intuitive knowing. Or simply: any inexplicable encounters with the unknown.

Whatever we call it, let's face it: magic is inconvenient to most folks, disrupts their daily routine, takes away from the enjoyment of a happy day, and generally disturbs and confounds their belief systems upon which has been built the immovable foundation for A Normal Life. Anything that does not align with the traditional status quo is therefore a pain in the ass, a thorn in the side, a discrepancy in the matrix, and something to be avoided at all costs. So now's the part where you stop and ask yourself - *Am **I** a pain in the ass to the world at large?* If you are reading this book, you probably already know the answer to that question.

As a child, I had many magical experiences. As stated in the introduction, I'm really not sure why the world of mysticism and magic seemed to single me out, except perhaps because I slipped through the cracks of traditional upbringing. Or, put another way, I was spared the dubious benefits of a lot of the programming which most children endure just by virtue of being alive. Living in an isolated rural environment with a mother who was at work from 6 a.m. until 6 p.m., and a father who was less than attentive, I more or less ran wild in the neighborhood in a time before fences or pit bulls. The swamp, the lake, and the orange groves were my milieu, and as an only child, my so-called invisible friends were my *only* friends.

It was idyllic.

In hindsight, I can also clearly see that the lack of traditional programming allowed my mind and spirit to develop in what I would consider to be a more natural fashion than most kids growing up today. With no television in the house until I was six, no telephone, no video games, no DVD or computer, *and very little adult supervision,* I was forced into a bond with the natural world and, ultimately, the supernatural world.

So the tales I tell here may sound like fanciful imaginings of an isolated little girl, remembered by an elder witch through the eyes of poetic license. If that's what makes you sleep better, then you are free to inject that belief into your own programming in the same way a doctor might inject morphine into the IV line of a patient experiencing a great deal of pain. The morphine doesn't really make the pain go away, of course. It only masks the symptoms, but for the most part, that's what patients are looking for. And it's what most folks are looking for in their day to day lives.

I'm reminded of Arnold Mindell's comments in his excellent book, *The Shaman's Body*. Even though I've quoted this passage more than once in my previous books, it is so relevant to the material presented here that it bears repeating.

> *Is it your fault if you remind others of dreams they do not want? And who can blame the group, either for resistance to you or for the life-and-death struggle that ensues? These people are fighting for their lives, equilibrium, homeostasis - indeed, for the perpetuation of history. "Do not disturb us more than we can take," they say.*
>
> *From a global viewpoint, you disturb your organizational system, and history must fight for continuity. In this universal and fated interaction, the warrior's friends become the voices of the web. Their warmth turns to ice. They accuse you of unjustifiable behavior, egotism, and criminality as they become possessed by their lawmaker role in this eternal drama of human*

history.

The collective you live in must pursue you for what it experiences as criminal acts and bring you to trial, just as you have challenged other rule breakers in the past. Now it is you who enters into a life-and-death struggle with the universe..."
                              -Arnold Mindell, *The Shaman's Body*

For those who have been engaging in the world of shamanism or magic for any length of time, it is almost a certainty that you, too, have been labeled as a pain in the collective ass of society, or even your own family and friends. If you have been on the path as long as I have, it is even a strong possibility that you are a lone practitioner now - for the ugly truth is that this path does not really make us many friends. We might connect from time to time with other warriors on a parallel path, but when we commit to this journey with the totality of mind, body and spirit, we quickly discover that in order to be true to ourselves, we can no longer uphold the expectations of others in the manner to which they have become accustomed.

What does *that* mean? "Surely you jest, Della!" someone is sure to say. "I have dozens of friends and a loving and supportive family, and I am still a warrior!"

Maybe.

My mantra is simple: *It. Has. To. Be. Real.* And it is when we begin to be absolutely true to the Self that we find ourselves out of step with the status quo.

What is the status quo? Greatly simplified, it is the consensual reality, in which there are rules and agreements we are all expected to live by. Which brings us to the issue of expectations. What is expected of us by our friends? Our family? Other warriors? And if we find ourselves leaning toward wanting or needing to satisfy those expectations, are we then attempting to mold ourselves into the consensual programs as a means to seek acceptance and that sense of well-being we are "supposta" experience when surrounded by family and friends?

Personally, I have come to see the expectations of others rather like individual bars on a cage. *How are you doing?* Fine, thank you (the expected response, when in reality you have a painful hemorrhoid and your dog won't stop humping your leg in public). *And how is your lovely wife today?* She's doing well, thanks for asking (even though she's on anti-depressants as a result of catching you in bed with the pool boy twice last week). *Would you like fries with that?* No, I'd prefer a dinner salad, thank you. (But you're lying and you know it. You want the fries. But you say the right thing because you're having lunch with your skinny friends who have been duly assimilated by the tao of lettuce[3].)

But I digress. Your painful hemorrhoid and your horny dog and your inability to keep your pecker in your pants are still foibles which polite society will agree to overlook in order to maintain their illusion of normalcy. After all, the priest may tell you we are only human with human shortcomings. Say a few Hail Marys, kick the dog out the back door, get some Preparation H, slap your errant prick into submission, and all will be right with the world. And who knows? In the world of matter and men, in the world of polite society, perhaps the preacher is correct to the extent of his understanding of the agreement. You may be an asshole, but you're a *normal* asshole - a card-carrying member of The Human Agreement.

But what if you were to be sitting there at lunch with all those malnourished normal friends of yours, and you just happen to casually mention during the appetizers that you were abducted by aliens last week. Everyone laughs it off, of course, because you are obviously joking around as you are wont to do, you little minx, but by the time that nasty-tasting dinner salad arrives, you've made a reference to a prophetic dream you had, and now the laughter is getting more nervous and your best friend's wife has dropped her fork with a loud

---

[3] http://www.quantumshaman.com/html/rant_lettuce.htm

clattering sound more than once.

When the main course is served, you turn the conversation toward the fact that your house seems to be haunted by the spirit of the former occupant, who appears in the mirror over your sink every other Thursday and whispers, "Cats really do go to heaven," in a melodic but androgynous voice. Now you're keeping in mind that these are your closest friends - maybe even people you grew up with, went to college with, friends with whom you have discussed all manner of philosophy at one time or another. Is there life on other planets? Is religion a comfort or a crutch? Did don Juan really exist, or was Castaneda just stoned on mushrooms and made the whole thing up? Was Nietzsche onto something with nihilism or is nihilism just much ado about nothing?

To you, these things are just a part of your inventory now, maybe even the fuel that drives your imagination. So by the time dessert arrives, you're talking openly about the projection of the shaman's double as a quantum vessel of energetic awareness, replete with free will and the ability to transcend the space-time continuum.

But what you have perhaps failed to notice is that your friends left Neverland long, long ago. They went away and grew up and got married and had lots of babies, so by this time, their amusement has turned to outright discomfort, and the males at the table have turned to talk of Nascar and beer, while the females have retreated to The Ladies Powder Room to do whatever it is females do in the restroom that seems to require at least half an hour and the assistance of their twelve closest friends.

You are alone.

In the middle of friends, surrounded by those closest to you...

You are alone.

Magic is a burden to others. At some point, this becomes obvious. If you are extremely fortunate, you find yourself merely alone and not hanging from some makeshift cross or secured to a handsome pile of very dry kindling while the stuffy magistrate recites the charges against you.

This is where the journey takes a sharp and dangerous turn, and you have some decisions to make that are going to be painful.

Do you really want to be a seeker at all if this is where it leads?

But, far worse, do you have a choice anymore, or have you already wandered past the point of know return?

The Infinity of Eternity

When I was about six, I remember lying on the slide of the old swing set in the back yard, gazing up at the late afternoon sky. In church that morning, as I sat swinging my legs over the edge of the hard wooden pew, feet not reaching the ground, the preacher had been saying something about eternal life. I hadn't paid much attention, but now, for no particular reason, the concept found its way back to me in somewhat altered form.

Eternity and infinity. I barely knew the words at six. It was a different world then, simpler in a lot of ways. But as I was looking up at that too-blue sky while the sun was setting and the redwing blackbirds were calling and the Florida air was still and heavy, I felt my mind wrap around those two words in a way that was instantly life-transforming.

An odd melancholy settled over me, but simultaneously a great joy and sense of wonder. I felt my awareness looking back at me from infinity, extending into eternity, and I was no longer a six year old child, but some peculiar field of awareness that had only placed itself in the body of that child for a brief time so that it might begin to understand itself from the perspective of eternity and infinity.

I remember lying on that slide for over an hour, until my mother called me in for dinner, and the jarring experience of going from the cool twilight into the heat of an old wooden house that had no air conditioning and would have fallen down had the termites stopped holding hands.

My heart has been in the infinite ever since that day.

―――

The Transparent Man

Circa ~1963

One of my earliest encounters with the ineffable came when I was in the safety zone of my own bedroom. But as any kid who's ever had a monster under his bed can tell you - there is no such thing as a safety zone when one is 8.

I had gone to bed at the usual time, then nodded off to sleep. Being a light sleeper even as a child, I awoke a few minutes later to the sound the parents moving around. The house was old, most of it having been original equipment on Noah's Ark. Ancient timbers creaked and groaned. Pipes growled. The shared bathroom was like a hallway between the two bedrooms, and it wasn't uncommon for both doors to be left open unless the room was occupied. Florida nights are hot and humid, and any movement of air is to be worshipped.

On this particular night, the door on my side was open, and when I woke up I immediately glanced toward my parents' room to see if they were still awake. *Something* had caused me to stir, but as soon as my eyes fell on the open door, I found myself completely unable to move other than to blink. In hindsight, many years later, I was duly informed that I was merely suffering from sleep paralysis and hypnagogic hallucinations, but I find that a rather complicated attempt to explain away the fact that there was a transparent "man" standing in the passageway between my bedroom and the bathroom. I was not *physically* paralyzed. I was being quite literally *compelled* by the unrelenting gaze of this "man".

He wanted me to look at him.

He wanted me to *see* him.

And he wanted me to know he was neither a hallucination nor a demon nor an angel nor any other quasi-rational explanation.

For what felt like several minutes, I lay there in my bed, terrified and unmoving, unable to look away. I cannot really say what he looked like, for I was *seeing* with the third eye far more than any physical vision. And then, very slowly, he seemed to dissipate - beginning at the feet and moving slowly upward, the transparent man vanished back into whatever world had spawned him, and as soon as he was gone I was once again able to move.

But I *didn't* move. I just lay there, staring at the space where he had been, wondering for a moment if my Crazy Granny had been right all along, if there really *was* a special fire just for me, and the transparent man was just the devil's minion sent to fetch the soul of one very bad little girl.

I knew better, of course. But that didn't bring me any closer to understanding *what* the transparent man might really have been. So I held my silence entirely, knowing that if I said anything to anybody, there was sure to be an investigation into the status of my sanity, and at the very least I would be dragged up in front of the hillbilly preacher to be tested for possession.

Life went on. I dreaded going to bed, because I did *not* want to see the transparent man again. Weeks went by, and then a few months. I began to feel safe. Even started to think maybe I *had* been dreaming, not because I believed that, but because it is human nature to explain away the things we don't understand, particularly if those things are frightening or not in alignment with what we tend to think of as 'reality.'

And yet...

Just about the time I was getting comfortable in my own skin again, I went to bed one night, had not even fallen asleep yet, and there he was again. In the doorway. As if he had been waiting for me to arrive.

As soon as our eyes met, I was once again immobilized. The only thing I could do was blink, but I could not look away. Because there was a wind-up clock in my bedroom, I was aware of the passing of time by *the tick-tock tick-tock* of the seconds of my life flying by. It wasn't so much that I was afraid of the transparent man. I was afraid of what was happening to *me*. Was I losing my mind? Was I dying?

I tried to speak and couldn't.

I tried to close my eyes but they would not close.

And then, as before, the transparent man just slowly dissipated until the room was once again empty, as if he had never been there at all.

As soon as he was gone, I gave up all ideas of being a good little girl and keeping my silence. Instead, I went howling and screaming into my mother's room like a demented banshee, telling the tale of a strange man in my room.

Glenn ignored me completely.

As for my mother, all the right things were said and done as prescribed to calm an hysterical child. She coddled me for a minute or two, then went and got the big orange flashlight from the kitchen, and proceeded to do a thorough search of every nook and cranny of my bedroom. I kept trying to tell her that the transparent man wasn't hiding under the bed or in the closet. He wasn't behind the curtains or tucked behind the door. He has simply folded himself sideways and beamed back up to whatever starship had sent him, or else he had turned to mist like the legendary vampire and wafted through the keyhole back into the night that never ends.

Of course, in those pre-*Star Trek* days, there was no such idea as 'beaming up', and I had never been exposed to even the vaguest idea of a vampire at that age, so I could only express myself in a little girl's language (albeit a bit excitedly at that point) while my mother stood there looking at me as if I were some quaint new species of ant that had crept in through the crack underneath the door.

When she pronounced that the room was "safe and sound," as if that were intended to make me feel better, I simply followed her when she went back to her own room, and spent the rest of the night curled up on the chair next to her bed.

As the two bedrooms were virtually identical, and as I would *not* sleep in that room ever again, the following day the furniture was switched and I took up residence in the back of the house rather than the front. I never saw the transparent man again (though one of my mentors once said emphatically, "You will.") I have never really known what he wanted, or if he might have been a mere visitor from some other place and time, looking for Platform 9 and 3/4.

One thing is certain, however. He is one of the defining events in my life - something my mind seeks out whenever I find myself unwittingly chained to the mundane. He is a reminder that *nothing* is what we have been taught to believe. He is an icon of the unknown. He is a self-replicating mystery in a world of mundane sameness.

Maybe that was his sole purpose all along. Who's to say?

It is interesting to note that, several years later, Glenn died in the room where the transparent man had appeared, and several months after his death, my mother reported seeing a man standing next to the front window. Even she acknowledged that it would have been impossible, since the house was at least three feet higher than the ground, so the "man" would have had to be at least ten feet tall.

Such was the nature of the house where I grew up and spent the first seventeen years of my life.

The Little Voices

January 19, 1973

I've always felt that the things which truly define us are the things that remind us "the world is nothing like we think" (and, therefore, neither are *we*.) The encounters with the transparent man were life-defining Events, in that it really proved to me that essentially *everything* I had been taught about reality was questionable at best.

I had been absolutely programmed *not* to believe in ghosts, or things of the otherworld, and I wasn't at all a fearful child, so there was no logical reason for the experience. And yet, it is one of those things I turn to in my mind and look at when I start to feel myself slipping into the clutches of the consensual agreement. It's like an island of the nagual in the churning sea of the tonal.

The morning my father died was another one of those defining Events. He always came in at 7:05 to get me up for school, but that morning he didn't come. I was secretly delighted and intended to stay in bed and just sleep, but then my Crazy Granny came pounding on the door with her cane and ruined my plans. I had every reason *to* stay home that day - cramps, already late, etc.

But all of a sudden there was a man's voice in my head that said, *Get out of the house! Now! Go to school! Get out of the house!* I had never heard that voice before, but I took heed, got up, got dressed, spoke briefly to The Old Man (who was still in bed, hands underneath the covers, probably holding the very gun that was destined to end his life later that morning). He was as close to normal as he ever was, and offered no explanation as to why he hadn't gotten me up as he always did. The exchange was no more than a few words, and then I walked the short distance to the bus stop and settled in for the 45 minute ride to school.

The morning was unusually dull somehow, crawling by in slow motion. Teachers stood at their stations, mumbling off equations and philosophical conundrums and reciting the Sonnets of Big Bill Shakespeare, but it was all like a bad black and white movie playing on the surface of the air.

It was close to noon when someone from the office came to the door of Mr. Connell's philosophy class and I was mysteriously summoned to the guidance counselor's office. It was there I was notified in a very succinct sentence that left no room for interpretation, "Your father is dead."

No details. The counselor drove me the 35 miles home. We spoke little, shared a cigarette, and watched the Florida swamp lands glide by in silence.

When I got home, I was told Glenn had committed suicide - a conclusion that is questionable in the aftermath of a massively botched investigation, but ultimately it made little difference in the grand scheme of things. Whether he killed himself or someone else murdered him, there is *no* doubt in my mind that I would have died, too, if I had remained at home that morning.

Glenn was the type who would have killed me to take me with him because that was his nature; and if it *wasn't* suicide, whoever killed him probably would have killed anyone else in the house, too. That voice in my head - undoubtedly Orlando - was one of those ineffable manifestations that still haunts me to this day, and has become one of those defining events that serve to remind us...

Nothing is what we have been taught to believe.

Gremlins, Goblins or Faeries?

~circa 1982

We were renting a house on the outskirts of San Diego. The community itself was relatively new, the house nothing special, and the day not particularly spectacular in any way.

It was a time when Wendy was still in college, I was working a shit job at the local K-Mart, and our third roommate was on an extended out of town trip. So when Wendy and I woke up that morning, there was nothing at all out of the ordinary. The house was in a state of disarray, for we had been collating a large underground press magazine, and so there were 8' long boards propped precariously on chairs in the kitchen and living room. Stray pages littered the floor and the two fat male cats were skating around in the chaos.

There was no time for anything other than a glass of orange juice and a shower, and then we left the house together, leaving the cats lounging in patches of sun streaming in through the large sliding glass doors. Wendy dropped me at K-Mart, then went on to what sounded like it was going to be a full day for her at college.

I was scheduled to work a full shift as customer service supervisor that day, which left me feeling less than enthusiastic. Nothing more fun than standing behind a counter where grumpy, demanding and often insane people come to return everything from sleazy lingerie (usually *used* sleazy lingerie) to open cans of dog food to items that were clearly stolen and now being returned in an attempt to cash in even further on their nefarious activities.

Never a dull moment.

At the end of my shift, a co-worker gave me a ride home, where I had expected to find Wendy waiting. Instead, there was a typed note left in my IBM Selectric which read...

> *I won't be home until late because I'm going to Michael D's poetry reading.*

The only thing really odd about the note was that I didn't understand why she hadn't told me when we left that morning, combined with the fact that the house was immaculate. The only conclusion I could draw was that she must have come home for lunch - the campus wasn't far from our house - and taken the time in between classes to thoroughly clean the house. Gone were the long boards and the stacks of paper, later found stacked neatly in the laundry room. The other peculiar thing was that the cats were nowhere to be found, but later turned up in the garage, safe and sound, but failing to understand why their favorite couch had not been delivered.

All of these things could be explained, and so I didn't think too much of it until Wendy came through the door shortly after 5 and remarked, "Wow - you cleaned the house!"

My head probably tilted like a confused puppy. "No, *you* cleaned the house, right?"

The conversation started off just like that. And then it escalated into what turned out to be our first major fight. She was adamant that she hadn't cleaned the house, and I was adamant that I hadn't done it, and before we knew it, we were at one another's throats like an old married couple.

In reality, of course, it was fear driving the train. If *she* hadn't done it and *I* hadn't done it, that only left... one helluva mystery and absolutely *no* rational explanations. Jim was out of town, on the east coast, as a matter of fact. And he would have grown wings and flown away before he would *ever* have done the kind of cleaning that had been done. It would have taken hours - everything from the tidied-up collating mess to several loads of laundry neatly folded and stacked.

We argued.

We fought.

Finally we found a precarious peace. Maybe there just weren't any answers. So we made a slippery truce and went to the grocery store together to find something for dinner. It was right about then that I remembered to ask Wendy why she hadn't gone to the poetry reading after all.

"What poetry reading?" she said somewhere in the snack aisle. "I never said I was going to any poetry reading today."

I reminded her of the note in the typewriter, only to be

met with the adamant insistence that she not only had *not* cleaned the house or locked the cats in the garage, and she *certainly* had not written any note and left it sticking in my typewriter.

So we argued some more.

And we fought some more.

And by the time we got home, we were on the verge of dissolving our relationship entirely, even though we had been together for a couple of years and had *never* had even the slightest inkling of an argument.

Once back in the house, I took the groceries into the kitchen and Wendy went to our bedroom in the back of the house. She returned a few moments later with a pink flower - still wet from the sprinklers and sporting a fine, fat ant - and a look on her face that spoke volumes.

"This was on the bed, between our pillows," she said.

At least we could agree that neither of us had put the flower there, since we had been together the entire time and it certainly wasn't there when we left to go to the store. With the house being as tidy as it was, we would have noticed.

We ate in silence that night. When we *did* find a sufficient balance to discuss what *might* have happened, it started to come down to the note left in the typewriter and what could have been some rather sinister implications. Normally I would have expected Wendy to be home around 5, but whenever she went to one of her professor's poetry readings, the evening could drag on until 10 or later. So we speculated as to what the agenda of the note-writer might have been. Was it meant to delay the time before I would even suspect a problem? In a day long before cell phones, there was no way to contact her and no reason for her to contact me, but even as we wracked our brains, we could come up with no logical reason for *any* of it.

We searched the house and garage. No signs of forced entry. No gremlins or gunmen hiding in the shadows.

The cats weren't talking.

Over the days and weeks ahead, the incident continued to haunt us in ways that came perilously close to ending our relationship. Wendy told her friends about the incident, and they pointed the finger squarely at me. I told my friends about the incident, and they pointed their finger squarely at her. Stalemate.

Wendy even went and talked to the neighbors, who had seen nothing - not a stray car on the street, not a passing ghost with a fetish for cleaning other people's houses, not a wayward little green man just looking to stir up mischief.

Over time, the incident slowly faded, though no real answers were ever found. Some have speculated that it was a case of mistaken identity, their argument being that a maid-for-hire service came to the wrong house and worked their magic while we were away. Others have suggested that someone solicited the services of a cleaning crew in the hopes of doing us a favor, never suspecting the amount of chaos and emotional upheaval it would cause.

The only problem with *that* theory (which I did actually consider) was that the cleaning crew certainly didn't sneak back in while we were at the grocery store and leave a pink flower on the pillow, almost as if to apologize for the ruckus that had ensued. *No* cleaning crew is *that* perceptive, especially since it would have meant someone was actually *in* the house at the time Wendy and I were arguing.

It remains a mystery.

When I've told this story at various gatherings over the years, I'm often asked, "What do *you* think happened, Della?"

To be honest, I have no idea. So many aspects of the whole thing are completely outside the realm of what we think of as possible. So what I *really* think is that *something* happened, but I will probably never know who or what it might have been.

———

The Blue Camaro

Circa ~ 1983

I was living in San Diego at the time. A good friend had just moved into the area, a young woman who had also had strange experiences all her life, and has since embarked on a deeply committed spirit quest of her own. My own life at that time was odd, to say the least, in that I had been surrounded by weird happenings since childhood, but had not yet been able to place them in any cohesive context.

I was in my mid-20s at the time, and to be candid, I had been literally chased, haunted and at times terrified by a series of ongoing manifestations. This often took the form of being stalked by a blue Camaro, occupied by two men who could *not* exist... but seemingly *did*. There were the nights of coming home late from work and being followed by the blue Camaro. The car was often seen in the parking lot of my work place, but by the time the police were called, it would conveniently vanish.

To answer all outstanding questions, *yes* I had taken all possible precautions. And *yes*, I knew even as it was happening that these events were not of the ordinary world, but manifestations of the unknown. *Because* of that knowledge, I was more intrigued with the blue Camaro and its occupants than afraid - at least that turned out to be the case after the first year or so of these uncanny occurrences which began in Miami and followed me all the way across the country when we moved to San Diego. Bottom line - if the occupants of the mysterious car had wanted to assault me or make a stew of my bones, there had been more than ample opportunity. The cats weren't trying to *catch* the mouse. They were just toying with it for reasons not clear at the time.

So on this particular afternoon, Dina and I had taken a walk down to a park at the edge of a canyon known locally as The Gorge because it was so deep and lush in comparison to most of the desert-esque landscape of San Diego. The park itself was on a cul-de-sac, about a block from my house, with the only access being across a narrow footbridge barely wide enough for a golf cart. The sun was just going below the horizon, but it was still full daylight, when all of a sudden I heard myself saying to Dina, "If a blue Camaro comes around that corner, we're going *thataway*!" I jerked my finger to the south, where several telephone poles had been rolled in a line to form a perimeter of the park to keep cars from driving onto the grass.

There was no reason whatsoever for me to say this, for I had never been pursued by this anomaly when in the presence of any other human being. It was one of those things that always happened when I was alone. So, I could only imagine I was imagining things when I heard a squeal of tires and looked up to see a blue Camaro rounding the bend in the cul-de-sac and coming at high speed toward the park. As mentioned, the only way in was a narrow footbridge, and though it had never occurred to me that anyone would be crazy enough to drive a car over it, that's precisely what happened.

Suddenly, instead of two young women walking in the park, we were two fluffy bunnies caught in the headlights. That's when the internal dialog stopped. I grabbed Dina by the arm and pulled her in the direction I had indicated earlier, and we took off running. At our backs, we could hear the car rattling over the wooden bridge and emerging onto the grass. Neither of us looked back as we leapt over the telephone poles and ran headlong through snake-infested brambles and thorny bushes which had grown up at the back fence line of the houses next to the park.

Run. Hide. Crouch down. Pure survival mode, with everything happening in slow motion until, eventually, we made it to the street on the far side of the field, and were able to walk the long way back to my house. The other odd thing is that the only way *out* of that cul-de-sac would have meant the blue Camaro would have to pass by us. It never did. When we got back to the house, we immediately got in my Mustang and went boldly and somewhat angrily cruising down to the park with the intention of seeing where the blue Camaro might have been hiding.

The tire tracks went right up to where we had jumped over the telephone pole... and then they just *stopped*.

Because the grass was thick, lush and wet, it was obvious it had never turned around. The tracks just *ended* there.

That experience is one of those things that still hangs in my mind as absolute validation of the machinations of the unknown. Not to mention a damn good exercise in stopping the internal dialog and running for your life.

But still...

I often wonder in years-long hindsight, what might have happened if we had stood our ground and waited to see who or what might emerge from that mysterious blue Camaro.

And then there is the question... Do we foresee events through telepathy or even remote viewing, or do we create reality with our thoughts, rather like the old *Star Trek* episode entitled *Shore Leave*? Did I foresee that the car was going to come around that corner, or did I create it with the thought that it might? Jury's still out.

"Shore Leave" Photo copyright © by Paramount Pictures

Left Turn at Wonderland

Circa ~1988

I suspect I was abducted by aliens as a child. Not because I remember it, but because I have an almost psychotic reaction to being poked, prodded or probed by any member of the medical profession for any reason. Sure, nobody likes going to the doctor, but this goes well beyond what we like or don't like. When I was maybe 7 years old and my mother was dragging me to the Nazi dentist with an office on the 10th floor of an old gothic-style building, I actually slipped my leash and climbed out on the window sill, where I sat with my tiny feet dangling over the edge until such time as I was coaxed back inside with promises of something that made life seem worthwhile. Don't recall what it was now, but suffice to say it did *not* get me out of going to the dentist who had apparently never heard of novocaine and also seemed to take great pleasure in drilling without anesthesia into the pulpy root of a tooth to the sound of screams. I tell ya, that fucker was a sadist, and that isn't a word I use lightly.

Yes, that kind of thing tends to make a child wary of doctors in a way that doesn't dissipate even when one becomes an adult.

The fact that I was 33 at the time this next incident occurred had done nothing to soften the intense hatred I had for dentists, yet I had nonetheless had to go to one that day to have an extraction. There was much poking and prodding. A lot of needles jabbing into sensitive and inflamed tissue, and finally a lot of yanking, pulling and excruciating agony that managed to sneak right past the novocaine and nitrous oxide.

To someone who has never experienced that kind of pain, it's not really possible to explain it, but the bottom line is that it results in an immediate and severe shift of the assemblage point. By the time the procedure was done and I was cleared to leave the office, it was late afternoon and my primary concern was heading home to the animals and having a good, long, self-pitying cry. Not my usual way of handling things, but there were a lot of other things going on at the time that had left me feeling displaced and disgruntled.

The drive home took only a few minutes, but when I turned onto my street, I felt a strange twinge of disorientation and realized the road was seemingly blocked about 100 feet before my driveway. But upon closer look, I saw the street wasn't *blocked* there. It simply *ended* there.

I could clearly see my house just a bit beyond where the pavement ended, but the only way to access it would be to go back to the main highway, backtrack to the nearest cross street, and come in another way.

The disorientation I was feeling at this point was profound - largely because I had left the house only 3 hours before and certainly there had been no evidence that the road was about to be permanently closed and a cinderblock half-wall installed where the street had once been. It also seemed rather odd that the wall was partially covered with a flowering vine that had apparently grown there and flourished instantaneously.

After backtracking and coming down the side street, I was able to get to my driveway, but mine was the only car where there were normally three - mine, Wendy's and our other housemate's.

By this time, the novocaine had worn off entirely, my mouth and jaw were throbbing, and I was still sporting a very large mad-on at the world as a result of being (yet again) poked, prodded, probed and pestered by (yet) another doctor.

So I stormed out of the car and up to the front door, only to realize it was a different color that it had been when I left the house. Obviously the other two housemates hadn't rushed off to the hardware store and bought a can of turquoise paint, so I began to wonder if I had somehow managed to end up in the wrong driveway on the wrong street at the wrong house.

And yet, that clearly was *not* the case. The address on the mailbox was correct. The flowers I'd planted not long ago were still blooming. Everything was as it should be.

Yet it was *nothing* like it should be.

My key didn't work the lock.

No one answered the door when I rang the bell repeatedly.

The cat in the window was not *my* cat.

A cold, sick feeling crept into my chest, and I remember standing there on the doorstep having the thought that I must have *really* fallen down the rabbit hole this time. I alternated between being angry and feeling sorry for myself, wondering if "they" had changed the locks and moved out just to ditch me, or if someone was gaslighting me just for a wicked laugh.

I waited for some jackass to leap out of the bushes to inform me I was on *Candid Camera.*

I laughed at myself for the absurd thoughts.

And yet, I could find no rational explanation. Where was my lover? Where was my house if not *here*? Where was **I** and how would I find my way back home?

After several minutes, I went back to my car and just sat there for quite some time. The horses and the pipe corrals were not in the back yard where they should have been - not even trampled earth that would say they had ever been there at all. The neighbors' houses all looked exactly the same as they had that morning. The old lady next door was out watering her geraniums. Everything *looked* altogether normal.

But wasn't.

Not knowing what to do, I was on the verge of outright panic when a very calm male voice I have since come to recognize as Orlando said, *Go back the way you came and take a walk in the park.*

At first, I wanted to protest, wanted to somehow *demand* that things correct themselves, or else make my way to the nearest nuthouse and sign myself in.

My heart was pounding.

And yet, there was something in that man's voice that calmed me. He repeated his previous command, and almost without realizing it, I backed out of the driveway and drove to a nearby park on a lake, where I spent almost an hour trying *not* to think about what*ever* it was that had happened.

After awhile, just sitting there on the grass watching the ducks chase after bits of bread thrown by picnickers, I got back in the car and drove home the way I always did.

When I turned onto my street, there was no low wall blocking the road, Wendy's car was in the driveway where it belonged, and the door was the same faded yellow it had been when I left home that morning. My key even worked the lock.

I started breathing again and went inside as if nothing at all had happened. Only the cat gave me a weird look, as if he alone knew I had been hopping dimensions - an activity normally reserved for cats alone.

I'm sure someone will say it was only the drugs administered at the dentist's office that resulted in a distortion of my perception. If that's what makes you sleep better, go right ahead and adopt that belief. I'm sure someone else will say I turned down the wrong street because residential neighborhoods in San Diego tend to look alike and obviously it was just a drug-induced error on the part of the driver. If that's what keeps your status quo intact, you're free to believe it.

All I know is that I was *there*.

What I *don't* know is which or what *'there'* I wandered into. It certainly wasn't the one with which I am familiar - and though it was terrifying at the time, I have learned to look at it with a sense of wonder and even awe. In the big picture, when no explanations are possible, we can either wage war with the unknown (and we will *always* lose that battle), or we can accept what mystics, scientists and quantum time slippers have known all along...

> *"The world is not only stranger than we imagine. It is stranger than we **can** imagine."*
>
> -Arthur Eddington

Sand Storm Time Trap

Circa ~Autumn, 1992

We hadn't been living in the desert very long - maybe a month or two - when I realized I could no longer procrastinate going down to Palm Springs for whatever it is one seems to need on a daily basis. Cat food. Dog food. Left-handed monkey wrenches. The Landers Earthquake had occurred while our house was in escrow, which meant the local K-Mart was neatly folded up into a pile of rubble where it once used to stand, and the nearest large stores were 35 miles "down the hill" as the locals say.

Even though I had been avoiding the trip for more than a week, I finally took it upon myself as an adventure, and set out one afternoon of absolutely no consequence whatsoever. It was the first time I had made the long drive (about 35 miles) and so I had no idea what to expect. At first, the descent from the high desert was uneventful, but as the white IROC-Z28 Camaro emerged from the canyon that drops down out of Morongo Valley, I was greeted by a full-on sandstorm and fierce winds blowing in from the pass.

It occurred to me that perhaps I should continue on to the I-10 and take the freeway, but I'd been told by numerous locals that "the back way" was much faster. So I took The Back Way.

The sandstorm had worsened by the time I'd driven only a mile or two, not to the point of threatening visibility, but it was certainly buffeting the car and undoubtedly sand-blasting a paint job I had labored to keep pristine. Still, it was enough of an adventure that I was secretly thrilled by the whole thing despite the fact that 18-wheelers and other high profile vehicles were pulled over to the shoulder, and soon enough, there was *no* other traffic on the narrow 2-lane road at all.

Once one turns onto the road that is considered The Back Way, it's approximately ten to fifteen miles of essentially nothing before one crosses the I-10 - or at least that was the case back in those days. A few scattered houses. A trailer park. Three jackrabbits and a coyote or two.

By the time I had traveled another few miles, the sandstorm had increased and was beginning to obscure the road altogether. Whereas the pavement had been typical rough asphalt before, it had begun to look like a dirt road - which I thought at the time was a result of sand being deposited by the relentless winds.

There was nowhere to go except forward, or stop altogether and wait for it to pass. As it might take hours, and as I had other things to do that day, and as I am a stubborn adventurer at times, I kept going despite the fact that there were no other vehicles in sight, and the terrain all around me had turned to a odd beige fog swirling like Dorothy's twister.

At some point, it began to occur to me that perhaps I had taken a wrong turn and really *was* on a side road somewhere on the outskirts of Nowhere. But I had made no turns. It crossed my mind that maybe those trickster locals had deliberately given me false directions to see where the silly gringo would end up.

So when I saw a gas station with an old Phillip's 66 logo peeking out of the churning haze, I whipped the car into the dirt parking lot. It seemed that the gas pumps were old and almost alien, though on the heels of that thought came the realization that the world was shifting toward retro. Maybe it was meant to be cool and trendy.

When I was able to open the door against the sheer force of the wind and went inside the station, it, too, was out of step with the times. But once again, I didn't think too much of for the same reason I dismissed the odd appearance of the gas pumps. Old wire racks sported a few snacks and chips, all in wrappers I didn't recognize; there was another display in the back with motor oil, but for the most part the station was bare, cold, and uninviting. Three young men stood near the front - the attendant behind his old-style Royal cash register, and the other two apparently locals with nothing better to do while the sand storm raged outside and had now completely obscured the windows until it seemed we were captured in a bubble of calm in an otherwise tempestuous sea of chaos.

One of the men had moved to the door and was peering out toward the parking lot. "What kind of car is that?" he asked, squinting.

"It's an IROC-Z-28 Camaro," I said automatically. Then, to the attendant, I asked, "Can you tell me where the I-10 is? I'm thinking I must have taken a wrong turn somewhere."

"The what?" the young man asked, genuinely perplexed.

"I-10," I repeated. "The freeway."

A blank stare - not rude or dismissive, just one that said he really didn't know.

"The interstate?" I tried, realizing that Californians called it a freeway, but almost every state referred to the super-highways as simply, the interstate.

The three men looked at one another as if they really did want to help me, but also as if I were some strange bug that had just crawled in seeking shelter from the storm.

I began to feel genuinely uncomfortable - the way one feels in a horror movie when it's obvious to everyone *but* the protagonist that they have wandered into The House of Ten Thousand Terrors.

So I made a joke of it, saying I probably shouldn't have smoked that joint (even though I hadn't smoked a joint in 10 years), and then I got back in the car and continued on in the direction where the I-10 damn well should have had the good manners to appear at any moment.

The sand storm continued as the old gas station slowly faded in my rear view mirror. I never did find the freeway, but in another few miles, I came upon an intersection that looked somehow more normal, and it was at that precise moment when the air cleared, the winds abruptly stopped, and the world righted herself like a dog shaking rain off its back.

I looked around to find myself in a mostly residential

area, with houses typical in design of Palm Springs. Other cars were coming and going, and as I stopped at a traffic light, I saw the street sign read "Indian Canyon." I was precisely where I thought I was all along. Hadn't made any turns at all since taking The Back Way, and yet I also most certainly had never crossed the I-10, nor had I encountered any of the other business establishments known to be in that area.

Though I could not even begin to comprehend what had just happened, I completed my chores for the day and made the decision to go home by the same route I had taken earlier. Maybe I even wanted to tempt the Fates.

The I-10 was exactly where it should have been. No mysterious sand storm came out of nowhere to blast open the door to some alternate or parallel 'past'.

Life went on.

Some time later, I was able to do some research which revealed that the freeway had indeed not been built through that stretch of the desert until sometime in the early 1960s. I was never able to determine if a Phillip's 66 gas station had stood by the side of a dirt road at the edge of The Twilight Zone, or if anyone bothered to report a strange car that must have looked, to them, like something out of a science fiction movie.

I cannot even begin to speculate what really happened that day. All I know is that a door to the unknown opened wide out there on that lonesome stretch of desert highway, and I was allowed to take a side trip into the ineffable that still haunts me to this day.

Even though I have traveled that road hundreds of times since then, both alone and in the company of others, that door has never opened again.

The Pumpkin, The Crib and The Red Hearse

March 6, 2003

When I'm observing inanimate objects, it's usually with certain expectations which may or may not be valid in the shaman's world. For example, I do not *expect* a rock to move, but in the shaman's world, there's nothing to say it can't. We program ourselves to have certain beliefs and expectations, yet those are only belief systems as long as we *agree* to them. Some folks can walk on hot coals; a monk was once observed levitating a coconut; it sometimes might seem that faeries have moved a pencil from where it was left on the desk last night. All these things are possible when the programs are shattered and we enter into what don Juan[4] called "the sorcerer's world".

I recently reread *Illusions* by Richard Bach. Some of the events described were mirrors of things I've done in my own life, and with some degree of regularity. A few years ago, when I was first beginning to *see* that the sorcerer's world existed, I began experimenting. One day on the way home, I said to myself, "Okay, Self, if we create our own reality, let's test it. I want to see a red hearse before I get home."

In the middle of nowhere, on a sparsely traveled desert road, this seemed highly unlikely. I had the thought, let it go, and went on with my journey with no expectations. I hadn't traveled more than a few miles when I came to a 4-way stop. There, facing me in the oncoming traffic lane was a hearse. It chilled me to the bone, for though it wasn't red, it was most definitely a hearse. I patted myself on the back and said, "Okay, but not *exactly* what I asked for." But then, as the hearse and I passed one another going in opposite directions, I noticed the license plate. 1RED338

So... the big *It* has a sense of humor. Not only was the

---

[4] Don Juan Matus - from The Teachings of Don Juan, by Carlos Castaneda. Throughout this book you will find references to Castaneda, nagualism, Toltec practices and other aspects of shamanism. I highly recommend Castaneda's works as a background for anyone on a serious journey of spiritual awakening.

word 'RED' in the license plate, but the number 338 has major significance in my life.

I repeated this experiment many times. Once on a freeway in San Diego, I said to Wendy, "I want to see a crib before we get to your mother's house." No sooner had we gotten off the freeway than I looked into a residential neighborhood to see an unassembled crib leaning against a garage wall. A few months later, mid-summer, I said to Wendy on the same freeway, "I want to see a pumpkin before we get to your mother's house." Again, we got off the freeway, and there sitting on the front porch of a house was a fine fat pumpkin. Nowhere near Halloween or Thanksgiving. Not pumpkin season. Yet there she sat. Might as well have been some grand carriage drawn by tiny mice who had transformed into mystical horses. Just a pumpkin on somebody's porch, and yet one of the finest manifestations of the unknown I had ever witnessed.

Another incident: driving through the desert, again in the middle of nowhere. By this time I'm getting a bit demanding with my manifestations. So I picked something *really* impossible. I said to my traveling companions, "I want to see a washing machine before we get home!" And so as we bumbled along the road where only chaparral and jackrabbits dare to dwell, we came around a bend in the road, and there on the side of the road sat not only a washing machine, but a washer *and* dryer. Sense of humor evident. A sign on them said, "Free." Not if *that* wasn't a message from the beyond, I don't know what it might have been.

Free. Free your mind. Free your spirit. Free your heart.

Lose all expectations and all things become possible. Lose all doubt and the impossible will occasionally even manifest right before your eyes.

Finally, on the way home from Encino, stuck in a major traffic jam on the 101 outside of Los Angeles, I turned to Wendy and said, "I want to see a lion before we get home." She shot me a dirty look, stuck in traffic as we were, and she at the wheel. The stench of diesel and brushfire choked the air. Red tail lights had formed a river of blood that seemed to stretch endlessly, clogged in freeway veins. I shut up and went back to contemplating the dust on the dashboard. In less than two minutes, we rounded a bend, and there, emblazoned across the horizon, was a *huge* sign made entirely of tiny white lights, cast in the shape of a lion's head. Stood about 50' tall. And as if I might miss it, directly beneath, also enlightened in huge, glowing white letters, *The Lion King*.

There have been many such incidents since embarking on this path. So many I cannot count them all. So many that all I can do is gaze in wonder at the earth, the red hearses, the pumpkins and the lion kings, and occasionally glance at the face in the mirror and wonder, "What *are* you?"

The answer is a work in progress, a mosaic of memories and mumblings, a strange tapestry of stranger events that really aren't strange at all once we finally accept that the magic is real. It's our consensual view of the world that's the ultimate illusion, the greatest lie.

We expect the coconut to hang on the tree, but we might just as easily redistribute its molecules to become a fine, fat pumpkin on a porch in San Diego. It's all just an arrangement of energy in the sorcerer's world.

The Waiting Room

July 10, 2007

It had been a long weekend. After so many years of doing these Renaissance faires as a merchant, it all starts to blend together, and at times I find myself not quite remembering what city we're in or what day it is. Most of the time, that's okay - it allows the internal dialog to stop almost naturally, and quite often I realize I am gazing up at the sky or watching the wind stir the leaves of the trees. Unless something happens to disturb me, I tend to exist in a state of almost perpetually heightened awareness - on the bridge between ordinary and non-ordinary reality. Prime real estate, if you ask me.

This is also true when driving home from these long weekends, particularly when I find myself alone in the motor home as I did on Monday morning. Because the vehicle is a noisy beast of burden, I don't often play music while driving, much preferring to let my mind create its own entertainment. So as we drove through north Escondido, through border patrol checkpoints and areas once-green but now scarred with the signs of more and more new housing developments, I realized I was communing with Orlando.

Can't really say what we were discussing, if anything, though the communion was pleasant and alluring. I was aware of other traffic moving past me as I crested a large hill outside of Escondido, when suddenly a small black boxy car - the type preferred by shaved-headed rudesters in the age bracket of 21-30 - went zooming past me at such a high rate of speed I was instantly jolted back into hyper-awareness. Because he cut me off, I was forced to slam on the brakes and swerve to avoid smashing him like a bug on the windshield.

What I could not have seen was that *another* rudester - probably "the other guy" with whom Rudester #1 was road-raging - was already moving into the same lane I had just swerved into, and the laws of physics being what they are (two objects cannot occupy the same space at the same time), I was pretty certain Rudester #2 was going to end up as a greasy red smear on the side of the motor home.

Somehow, though, the collision didn't happen, and both rudesters went racing off in the direction of the wind when I suddenly found myself out of body in a manner that tends to happen in moments of great danger. Much to my surprise, it was not much different from this world. I was in a nondescript house, with a sense of being in an upstairs bedroom. The walls were grey-white, no decorations that I could discern, silver-grey carpets, and one window that faced north. The only furniture was a king-size bed with a white chenille spread, and a single nightstand where a pile of old hardcover books was stacked at least two feet high.

All of this I observed in a split second, as I became aware that Orlando was standing next to the bed, dressed in jeans and a long-sleeve white shirt, arms folded over his chest as he regarded me with a knowing little smile that was almost sinister. Just seeing him in that manner brought my heart into my throat. I wondered briefly if that collision had happened after all - if not in ordinary awareness, then certainly in some parallel reality.

Was this all there was? Just a nondescript room in a nondescript house on the edge of nowhere in particular? And the Nagual man standing there like some dark spirit of a night that will wondrously go on forever? Despite the fact that it had been daytime in the motor home, it *was* night here - black silk velvet, with a star hanging on a thin thread in the open window.

As if hearing my thoughts, Orlando laughed. "This is just the waiting room," he said with a shrug. "When I'm not manifesting as a little boy in Greece or a pirate on the old seas, or a prince in the leg irons of responsibility, this is as good a place to wait as any."

I didn't need to ask what he was waiting for. I had almost just experienced it - that last dance with the eagle that may come in the form of a car wreck or a heart attack or simply closing one's eyes and never waking up. I didn't bother asking if I were dead. Didn't seem to matter much, either way. To my amusement, I was okay with that.

"So what next?" I asked, sitting on the edge of the huge white bed. The chenille was soft against my palms, every bit as real as anything in ordinary awareness. He knew what was on my mind, but I spelled it out for him anyway. "Just seems these past few months haven't exactly gone according to plan.

And frankly I've even started to question the path. We like to think things happen for a reason, but the only meaning is what we assign to it all, and the only path is the one behind us."

Though he had been standing by the bed, I realized he had moved to the window. I say "moved" because that's how my ordinary awareness mind defines the results, but the reality of it was that he had simply shifted his assemblage point from A to B. No real movement occurred in the traditional sense.

It made me smile. So he stood there at the window with his back to me, gazing out at the vast expanse of infinity while his chest rose and fell as if he were just an ordinary man.

What he said next rattled me to the core of my foundation. "You've come to the end of the path." Now he turned and met my eyes, and in his gaze were galaxies and universes and entire vistas of the infinite glittering like diamonds just out of reach.

I forced myself not to look away even though it was like gazing into the depths of the abyss itself. I was reminded of the first time I spoke to this "man" when he was in manifestation almost 20 years in the past[5]. He had scared me then. He scared me a lot more now. And yet, at the same time and in the same breath, I was without fear, for none of it mattered anymore.

"Creation rises out of the nothing at the command of those who follow no path, you see. Every action you have taken on the journey has led you to this moment, when the road disappears beneath your feet and you realize it has led you to the source of all power, and that source is only yourself." Though his words held a twinge of melancholy, the irony appeared to amuse him. "What you do next is a matter of intent - but far more importantly, it is a movement of *Will*."

And then, before I could argue or agree or even think, I

---

[5] http://www.quantumshaman.com/html/mirror.htm

was back in the world of real time, on a freeway that was too brightly lit and too noisy and far too coarse and vulgar somehow. The motor home was still lumbering down the road, the rudesters were long gone, and for a strange moment outside of time, it was as if I were looking at a movie playing out on the windshield: two-dimensional, flat-line, unreal. A quick vision of *The Matrix* reminded me of the character who, after a lifetime of staring at it all, only saw the coding.

I realized that's how I have felt for quite some time. Having stripped away the illusions and the programs and the role-playing games, we are left with the code that runs it all, but appears to have no real source other than the code itself. Suffice to say that the coding is every bit as visible as the sunrise, and every bit as predictable. It's why I have been able to predict every unpredictable turn of events that has occurred over the past few weeks, and it is in the coding itself that I begin to realize why I have felt powerless at times to alter the course of that coding in my own life.

What you do next... is a movement of Will.

That movement of will has to do with operating at a level above or beyond or simply aside from the code. For as long as we are part of the code, as long as we are stuck on any "path", we are not truly free to create from the heart of the unknown. As long as we are part of the code, we are playthings of the eagle, extensions of the mundane world of muggles, phantoms and fools.

Over the days that followed this incident in the waiting room, I thought at length about Orlando's words. When we come to the end of the path, we begin to see that each of us is The One.

What's next is always what we create.

———

We Occupy the Same Space

A few years back, Wendy and I had gone out to dinner with some acquaintances, and I decided to return to the car to wait while they were reminiscing. Just felt a need to be solo for awhile, particularly since one of the attendees at the table could do nothing but talk talk talk, jibber jabber jabber jibber, saying absolutely nothing while nonetheless painting the air a tapestry of incompatible colors with her unasked-for observations absolutely everything from the beginning of time until its inevitable end. As I've progressed along the path, living a life not unlike a hermit for at least four months of the year in our winter downtime, I have come to loathe mindless chatter, preferring instead the concert of the Nothing, the orchestral serenity of silent knowing.

In the car, I dozed intermittently, then opened my eyes into full awareness. My head happened to be turned toward a low-rise hotel, and I was completely aware of my surroundings. But instead of the hotel as it should have appeared, I realized I was looking at a very old building. It was the *same* building, but seriously aged, dilapidated.

Because I was keenly aware of my surroundings and knew I wasn't dreaming, I made the decision to maintain the vision for as long as I could. I began studying the building, and observed that there were lights on inside the rooms, but the color and intensity said they were candles, like lanterns.

As I was studying this, an androgynous voice made the statement, *We occupy the same space, but not the same time.*

I was filled with a sense of awe throughout the experience, which I was able to maintain for approximately two full minutes.

What does it mean? Who's to say?

Just an unexpected but strangely pleasant encounter with the unknown.

Gabriel's Horn

As a child growing up in a dilapidated motel owned by my parents, we lived with my Crazy Granny, who was senile more or less from the time I was born. My memories are of her sitting on the porch in a rocking chair, literally waiting for Gabriel's horn. While waiting, she sang old hymns (mainly *Amazing Grace*), and talked in that 3-minute loop common to the demented and the elderly, wherein her entire existence could be summed up in these experiences that were all that seemed to remain of her memory. She spoke of Gert and Winnie, neither of whom I ever met, and who may have been nothing more than her invisible friends. And she spoke a lot to God and Jesus, asking them to take her home even though she would also proclaim in the same breath that she didn't want to die. Maybe she was hoping to be beamed up while still in her human garb, rather like Ezekiel and his fiery chariot. Who's to say?

Whenever I came home from school, I would ask how she was doing, and listen to the loop, which always concluded with, "And now I'm a-sittin' here, a-waitin' for Gabriel's horn."

Being a somewhat devious child, I had an instinct that she wasn't as daffy as she was trying to get everyone to believe, so one afternoon I crawled underneath the porch with one of those plastic flutofones from 3rd grade music class, and just as she was praying for Gabriel to sound his horn... I let 'er rip!

Toot-toot-ta-toot-atoot!

Next thing I know, I hear a clatter and a howl as Crazy Granny topples over backward in her rocking chair, feet up in the air like some deranged cartoon character, and all the while praying at the top of her lungs, "Jesus is coming! Jesus is coming!" as she tried to scramble up and right herself lest Jesus catch a glimpse of her size 10 bloomers which had been revealed when her faded cotton dress flew up over her head.

Needless to say, when I crawled out from under the porch, I wasn't the most popular kid on the block with my mother, but when I locked eyes with Granny and she realized that Gabriel was none other than her toe-headed granddaughter, there was a new understanding between us.

From that day forward, she had more lucidity when talking with me privately - in other words, she really *could* carry on a conversation beyond that 3-minute loop, though she would fall right back into it whenever anyone else entered the room. My guess was that she was bored with life and with the lives of those around her, and so she was recreating the reality that had been far more real to her - those 3-minutes of memories when she was really Awake, Aware and Alive (the 3 "A's). It's been suggested that perhaps Gabriel's flutofone shifted her assemblage point, but I would not want to take credit for the workings of an archangel.

Once, a few years before she died, I asked her what she really thought when she heard that horn sound. She just smiled. "There's a special fire just for you," she said, shaking her bony finger. "The devil has a *special* fire, just for you."

The Evil Butterfly of Interconnectedness

September 15, 2004

    Got home late from a long weekend of work. Detached the cargo trailer from the Suburban, had a bottle of water, then got back in the car to take our employee home, some 35 miles away. Was contemplating the idea of interconnectedness. Flow. Flow. One into the next. All into the each. Each into the other. Harmony and soft melodies swelling through a forest of tall pines where a young virgin blows kisses to a white unicorn. Ain't it all grand?

    Well... this morning I woke up and realized I needed something that was still in the heavily-loaded car. Ah, but in order to reach the items I needed (2 very heavy tubs), it was necessary to first unlock the trailer to search for the hand truck, which entailed finding the keys, which had been put back in the wrong place, and that meant stopping everything I was doing to initiate The Search. Once found, I unlocked the trailer to discover a veritable mountain of manna scrambled into a pile of rubble because the load had shifted in the 500 mile trip, so that meant methodically unloading each little trinket and putting it back in its place. This took about an hour in the desert heat until such time as I finally came upon the one item I had been searching for - the invaluable hand truck.

    By this time, my meditations on the subject of interconnectedness had begun to take a dark turn. I scowled, bared a fang, but continued with cussed diligence, muttering under my breath about the requirements of impeccability and the need to erase self-importance. Wiped sweat from brow. Rolled hand truck back to car, only ran over foot once (which required a trip to the head for a bandaid) and then realized that the items in question were buried underneath "The Fragile Stuff".

    Thinking again of interconnectedness. The dolls are connected to the fairies which are on top of the glass baubles, and isn't it lovely how it all forms such a splendiferous mountain of meaningless folly, but nonetheless is interconnected to my ability (or seeming lack thereof) to accomplish the *one* single task I set out to do in the first place.

In the course of making 25+ trips in and out of the house to unload each thing in accordance with its nature to break, scratch or suffer terminal damage [Note to Self: "I don't do delicate!"], I noticed that the path to the storage room was blocked by still more stuff which had been left in a state of disarray. This was discovered quite abruptly when, while carrying something that obscured vision, I tripped over aforementioned chaos, banging shin severely in the process. Another trip to the head, another bandaid, then back to the storage room to face the original disarray, plus the added bonus of all the stuff dropped when leg was nearly fractured. Cleared path, took deep breath to cleanse the spirit, inhaled large amount of dust, sneezed violently, wrenching neck in process

grumble grumble interconnectedness my ass

Finally unloaded the two tubs, but before I can get them in the house, the phone rings, so must run to answer the call; and the cat is giving me that look that says she's going to do something foul if I don't change her box *right now*. The one normally-flat surface in the house (the bed) looks like two bigfoot mated there, and before I can use it to sort through all that "fragile stuff" which is now being carried around by the weenie dogs, I have to strip off the sheets and throw them in the wash (because one of the weenie dogs barfed on the comforter), but there's a huge box on top of the washer which has to be moved first, which means throwing the sheets on the floor (can we all see this coming?), and that means tripping over them in the dark hallway. Another trip to the head. No more bandaids, the gun is out of bullets so can't shoot self, and by now the cat has reached the end of her patience and, yowling triumphantly, has deposited a token of her displeasure on the floor somewhere in the general vicinity of the litter box, but not exactly *in* it.

Another deep, healing breath - serious mistake. There *is* a devil. Cat poop is proof. My eyes water, blinding me to the table which has been moved in the brouhaha. Stub toe, thinking fondly of the butterfly flapping his wings in China to create a storm on the other side of the world, and by this time I'm seriously considering squashing the little fucker with a fly swatter, because all this interconnectedness is altogether true, but not all the sweetness and light it's cracked up to be. That butterfly is the incarnation of pure evil, and not all encounters with the unknown are mysterious and uplifting. Some are just plain annoying little lessons that choose the most inopportune times to reveal themselves.

Interconnectedness. Pffft.

By now, the weenie dogs are yapping for breakfast, but there's no dog food in the cupboard because the house sitter didn't bother to go to the store *or* inform me he hadn't done so, so that means a trip to Wal-Mart... in the car... that is still heavily loaded... with all that junk... which is interconnected to the last nerve... which is seriously frayed and beginning to unravel like a strand of cheap beads.

Om.

SHAMANIC DREAMING

Some would say that shamanic dreams are lucid dreams, and while that *can* be true, not all lucid dreams are shamanic dreams, and not all shamanic dreams are lucid dreams. Some also say they have shamanic dreams every night, at will, but that has not been my experience. Shamanic dreams come when they are most needed and contain some manner of lesson or symbolism. I've recently had two dreams that I would consider to be shamanic dreams, and both of which were undoubtedly direct interfaces with the infinite.

~

Tree of Stars

The dream:
I find myself on a train with a small boy, perhaps 8 years old, whom I know to be myself, though he is in separate manifestation, and "I" am his double - a man who would look in the mirror rather like a young Kevin Costner. As we are riding in the car together, the boy points to an upcoming stop and tells me, "That's where I used to live. Get off here and go take a look at the Christmas tree underneath my house."

Because the boy commands it, and there is all of eternity in which to move around, I get off the train and go to his house; but because it is night, it is only a dark structure against the darkness. No one lives there anymore, and so I sneak through an open window and drop down a chute into the darker darkness of what I know to be the underworld - a shamanic milieu often utilized in journeying. The blackness here is serenely and sublimely black, the shiny velvet canvas of the dark between the stars. The air is cold, crisp, and ever-winter, and snowflakes drift around me without touching me.

I walk a short distance until I come to see the tree the boy had spoken of. It is approximately 30 feet tall, nothing but dead twigs and dormant branches, yet it is shaped like a traditional Christmas tree, and the tip of each branch is a brilliant point of white light. Contrasted against the absolute darkness of the underworld, it is a magnificent sight indeed, and I am filled with awe and wonder.

As I stand in the blackness observing the tree, I see movement behind the trunk, and a small being emerges. About 3 feet tall, he is a shade of ochre like red clay, and somewhat misshapen, as if molded by a child's hand and not entirely symmetrical. He has a longish, pointed nose, and moves forward into the light of the tree, resting on his haunches as he looks at me.

I have no fear of the being even though I intuit that he is extremely powerful. He sees me in the darkness and begins to speak. "We have some concerns," he tells me, addressing me by a name I know to be my own, yet not a name I can bring back to waking awareness. I ask him to express his concerns. He replies, "Though ye be one of us, head of the table of us, ye went the way of the Moulie (a word which means 'the humans'). We fear ye will bring them here." By his tone and the back story which came with my "memories", I recall that I am indeed a being of the underworld, an extremely powerful one, in fact.

I look at the little being and *know* him, feeling compassion for him. "You needn't worry. It is not my intention to bring the humans here, but to show them the door to the Next World. Their evolution is not in this direction."

The little being seems relieved, yet sad at the same time, for it seems to indicate that even though this was my home and he was an ally and a friend, I will not be returning to this place anytime soon, if ever. As he sits underneath this tree of light, he is chewing on a blade of grass, which he reaches out across the expanse of the darkness to hand to me. A silent communication passes between us. If I eat the grass which grows beneath the Tree of Stars, I will be able to come back here if "the Next World" rejects me.

So I take the grass from his hand and chew it. It is sweet and earthy, and when I look at the Tree again, I realize it is all the constellations seen in the night sky. Orion and the Pleiades and Taurus and The Twins.

And then I am awake, back in bed as the last of the twilight fades from the purple horizon and a fine mist of rain dusts the window. It is dusk - the crack between the worlds. And I have seen the Tree of Stars and eaten the food of the immortals.

It is a good day.

Carlos and the Witch

In Dreaming: (February 28, 2005)
　　Spent the night with Carlos Castaneda. In the dream, I am in a small town in northern California, going from door to door taking applications from people, having something to do with refinancing their homes. An odd setting for a dream, since I have not been involved in real estate in many years, nor have I ever lived in northern California. Primarily, I am focused on one block, where there is a strong sense of community.

　　As the day winds down, a street party seems to spontaneously erupt. Many people have their garages open, and folks are dancing, having a good time. I am in someone's garage, brightly lit, surrounded by strangers in party mode, when a thin man with dark hair comes in and we make eye contact from across the room. Though I do not recognize him, someone tells me, "Oh, that's Carlos Castaneda. He lives here." The inference was that he lived somewhere in the town, not in that particular house.

　　He walks over to me and we begin talking. He is asking me about my double, about Orlando, and the conversation is very friendly. At one point, he says, "Can you show me?"

I ponder this for a moment, then extend both of my hands toward him, palms up - offering a sharing of energy. In the context of the dream, I intuit this to be something like the Vulcan mind meld.

He places his hands palms-down over mine, and his energy is very warm, but he doesn't seem to have the "power" to actually sink into me, so he takes a step back and motions to a woman I have not seen before. When she comes into view, she is very much like a traditional witch - extremely wrinkled skin, weathered and withered, with long, unkempt white hair. At this point, I am lying in a relaxed position on my back, and the witch comes over to me, takes my hands, and begins trying to get inside me on an energetic level. But unlike Carlos, her intentions are not benevolent, her methods harsh, cold and aggressive.

As this is occurring, I am calm and peaceful inside myself, thinking, *Does she really think she can steal my double*? It is preposterous to me, and I am both amused and a bit annoyed. By now, the witch is straddling me, and has placed her hands over my heart. I feel a powerful movement of energy, but again I am without concern - perhaps a twinge of dark curiosity - but then I feel the energy settle back into me, powerful and alive, untouched by the extremely cold pull she was attempting to exert. I sense Orlando within me, watching, amused.

At this point, the witch stands up and trades looks with Carlos, who was standing off to the side, observing. He laughs, then takes my hands and pulls me to my feet, embracing me. The witch also laughs and joins in. The inference is that I passed some test.

At this point, Carlos asks me if I could have Jeff do him a favor. I realize he is talking about a young man I knew years ago, and at first I say, "Sure, I'll ask him." Then, abruptly, I remember. I tell Carlos, "I'm sorry - obviously you don't know. Jeff died in a car accident several years ago." In the context of the dream, it never occurs to me that Carlos himself died, too.

The dream concludes as I leave the party and go out onto the road at the edge of town. The road is dark and filled with potholes as I stand at the crossroads. The road to the left, leading *up* is filled with wide gaps and cracks and looks as if it hasn't been traveled in years. Trees hang low. A branch strikes me in the face. I hear music coming from higher up on the trail. The other fork in the road is overgrown with bushes and foliage, so low I would have to stoop or crawl on my knees. The road on the left appears to circle behind the town. The road on the right leads away from the town.

I begin running up the road on the left, then stop. The music is coming from the party in the town, I realize, and so I decide to return to the party for awhile longer. Must admit, there was some fear in looking at the steep, dark road leading *up*. The road to the right was never an option; it appeared to be blocked altogether.

Returned to the town and the party, but decided to fly in just for the hell of it. Landed near a picnic table where Carlos was sitting talking to some shadows. He seemed surprised to see me, but pleased. For the time being, I was happy enough to spend the night talking with him on his picnic bench, knowing I would depart in the morning, "when the party is over."

~

So I spent the night with Carlos, was molested by a witch, and didn't take the high road when I could have. In waking awareness, I am wondering if the witch was actually a healer working on the heart chakra, because perhaps the most intense moment of the dream was that profound shift of energy I experienced when I felt her hands over my heart. Nothing was taken or given, but something *moved*.

In hindsight...

It's interesting to note that I had not experienced heart

problems at the time of this Dreaming. However, in 2010 I was overcome with an intense bout of angina which landed me in the hospital for three days. In August of 2014, I suffered a "fatal" heart attack while up in Washington. It is considered a miracle that I am still alive at all, and there are some strange tales to tell about the near death experience, as well as other aspects of the entire affair. After four days on full life support, I returned to awareness with two stents in my heart and absolutely no memory of the dream revealed above. In hindsight, I can only wonder as to the true purpose of the witch's Intent.

———

Fever Dreaming

Occasionally, if we are both fortunate and diligent, we might encounter an ally in Dreaming. I'm often asked - What _is_ an ally? In my experience, allies are inorganic beings who have as one of their agendas a desire to assist humans in their evolution. While there are other allies who might be more accurately described as obstacles, the ones I've met thus far have been both benevolent and extremely helpful.

~

January 9, 2005

Rain scratches at the window above my head, and the room has transformed to a purple egg in which I toss and turn, halfway between sleep and waking, a feverish traveler through the crack between the worlds. Time is nothing more than a line drawn in the sand. Free will enables me to step over it, beyond it, or erase the line altogether.

I sit up to see that this bedroom is not what I thought it was in waking life. An endless array of halls leads in and out, some well lit, others dark. I touch the sides of the egg and it becomes illuminated - pulsing, producing a soft humming sound like a slow, electronic heartbeat.

For a century or two, I drift in and out of otherworlds. "Tortoiseshell sunglasses are coming back in style," I'm told, though the message seems to have little significance and only makes me smile, even though I am shown a factory in China where thousands of workers are assembling next year's manufactured fad.

It's all illusion, I whisper. But no one hears.

Back inside the egg, I am fascinated with the long corridors coming into the room - entrances and exits I cannot recall ever having seen before. In one of them - a corridor in half-light, dusk-light, twilight - Orlando emerges in a fine Armani tux, carrying a black wedding cake, which he holds out to me in offering. At his back, deeper in the shadows, another man waits - a man I intuitively know to be Wendy's double.

For a moment or ten, I can only be amused, sitting there in inside the egg of my delirium with my legs curled under me, foolishly feeling safe despite the fact that my double is standing in front of me, dressed to kill and bearing a gift symbolic of so many things he has said in the past.

> *Let me court you and let it be slow and easy. My caresses will come and my fatal kiss will follow, but I am as hungry for the long slow dance of Life itself as you are hungry to be in my arms. This is how we feed one another, bride and groom, symbiots at our rehearsal banquet. Our wedding cake will be black, for that is the color of creation from which all things become manifest. I will feed it to you from my heart.*

Words written nearly a decade ago come back to me as clearly as if just having read them, and some little voice from outside the egg whispers, *Time is an illusion, too. You are already dead and forever alive. The immortals are laughing at your naïveté.*

In some other world seemingly disconnected by a thousand light-years, I hear a sound which I recognize as my own labored breathing, and at the same time I am seeing how fragile it is.

Between one breath and the next, eternity waits.

"I want to grow old on a serene front porch with Wendy at my side, an old dog at my feet and a couple of calico cats in my lap," I hear myself say.

Orlando smiles mischievously, dipping one finger into the thick black icing, touching it to the tip of his tongue. Might as well be the serpent and the apple.

"Life is but a dream," he tells me with tenderness and affection. "When it is time to awaken, the egg will dissolve."

And then it was night for a long, long time.

Dreaming Time

I lay in bed gazing at the rock wall above the fireplace, shifting the assemblage point from the world of ordinary awareness to a dreamer's, allowing the mind, body and spirit to align with Intent.

What surprised me was that almost immediately I found myself deep into Dreaming - yet I was still awake. I have never quite experienced this position of the assemblage point previously. Full dreaming, including visuals, lucidity, etc., yet at the same time a dual perception that I was still very much awake and still gazing at the rock wall. At first, the awareness of this unusual state brought me back to ordinary awareness, but with very little effort, I once again sank down into the state of dreaming-awake.

It wasn't long before I encountered a man in my Dreaming - one I knew to be a teacher. Without allowing my mind to drift, I said to the man, "Tell me about time." In the past, I have had dream guides tell me that humans simply do not comprehend the nature of time, and so we are stuck in it. So I made it my task to at least try for a better understanding.

The man - who was standing somewhere between the fireplace and infinity, in the terrain of dreaming yet the awareness of waking - regarded me briefly as if attempting to decide what to do with me. Finally, he said, "You humans need time and so you create it as a milieu or a platform, a stage on which events play out in such a fashion that they can be planned, experienced and then examined." He hesitated for a moment, and I could tell he wasn't satisfied with that explanation. "The problem, you realize, is that I am attempting to tell you about time while on that very platform, and so the explanation is rooted in words and symbols which add to the creation of time rather than doing anything to aid in its disenfranchisement."

I drifted in and out of dreaming. The man left me after that, and I saw an old woman who appeared haggard, old, and tired. No one I recognized, yet every woman, perhaps. The crone in her final days. Wise, and yet a prisoner of her body. She did not speak, but I saw that she was also a passenger on the time train.

~

I've had experiences, particularly on the mushroom ally, wherein time is perceived altogether differently than it is in ordinary awareness. We're still attached to the meat suit, and the only thing that has altered is perception - so I have to conclude that it is really only our perception that creates time and governs it to a certain extent. As children, time is also very different than it is as we grow older. As a child, it was an eternity from one Christmas to the next, yet as an adult, I honestly cannot account for the time that has passed from January 1 until the present. Literally, it seems no more than a couple of weeks ago that I was sitting at my desk, wrapped in a blanket, shivering from the cold. Now, with very little sense of time passing, I sit here in front of a fan, overwhelmed by the summer heat. The earth has tilted and the quail have hatched their young, but other than that, nothing appears to have changed. Where is "time"? In the tilt of the earth? In a bird's egg? In the force of gravity, as one of the little voices once suggested?

A few strange facts I've gathered with regard to time.

People living in colder climates have longer lifespans.

All lifeforce is suspended at absolute zero (about -432 degrees Fahrenheit).

As an object accelerates to near the speed of light, relative time slows down or stops altogether.

If I put all of that in a blender and swirl it around, it still comes down to perception, yet it may also have to do with being earthbound - because the conditions required to slow down or stop time exist naturally in outer space, in the absence of gravity and light. In the void between galaxies.

No conclusions, just ingredients in the mix. Just not sure yet if the mix is a cake, a pie, or a meatloaf.

And - yes - absolutely, those moments of being outside of time do indeed reveal to the seeker what it is to transcend the prison of time. I sometimes wonder if the whole reason we climb inside these meat suits is to motivate ourselves to evolve beyond the need for them. We may have to come into matter before we can inhabit the totality of ourselves through the double. Without the powerful motivation which is the awareness of our own mortality, there might not be sufficient cohesion.

It is through mortal life that we find the reasons and the means to transcend even time.

———

Karma who?

A seeker asked:
Is there such a thing as justice/karma or is the universe completely amoral?

I personally have seen no evidence to support the idea of karma as it is commonly (mis)understood, and in my opinion, the universe itself is entirely unconcerned even with our very existence. In that regard, it is more like the stage upon which we walk, a setting rather than a character. For it to be moral or amoral would imply a sentience at some level, and other than the ascended sentience of all those singularities of consciousness, I've seen nothing to indicate that the universe even notices we are here at all.

To me, the idea of karma is a scapegoat for people who want to blame their woes or attribute their good fortune to something other than their own actions in the Now. Granted, the actions we take in the Now will certainly have consequences in the future (and, to a sorcerer, even in the past, through retroactive enchantment), but in the quantum vision of it all, this can all be tracked straight back to the individual herself.

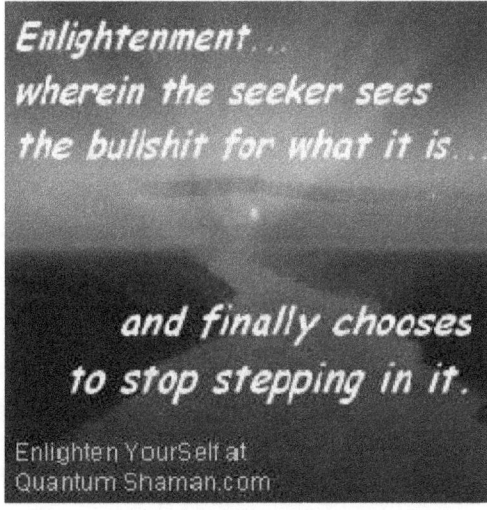

With that said I must admit with a paranoid grin that sometimes the universe does seem to be out to get me. Or, on the opposite side of the coin, I will have incredible runs of good luck. So while I don't attribute it to karma, I do see evidence for what I can only call a flow of energy in a specific direction.

Chances are if I stub my toe first thing in the morning, I will hit my funny bone in the afternoon and fall on my face before the day is done. If I wanted to attribute it to karma, I could perhaps say it was because I lied to my mother at the age of 6, but more likely, I'm just a klutz who wasn't being impeccable. I've said in the past that one definition of impeccability is learning *not* to crap in one's own path. Therefore, karma seems to me to be nothing more than what happens when we step in our own leavings. Nothing cosmic about it. Just cause and effect.

Does the existence or nonexistence of justice mean anything in terms of our relationship with our double?

Not as far as I'm concerned. This would take volumes to really explain, but let's just say there was a time when I felt I didn't "deserve" Orlando. I have certainly not lived the life of any sort of saint, nor even been a particularly good person at times - at least not insofar as the consensual agreements are concerned. I've lied to get jobs I wasn't qualified for (but which I knew I could do and *did)*; I shoplifted at the local gas station when I was a kid; and I once hid underneath the front porch where my Crazy Granny was waiting for Gabriel's horn, and tooted on a flutofone so loud that the old lady went tumbling out of her rocking chair with her feet sticking straight up in the air.

If there was any sense of cosmic or karmic justice, I certainly would not have deserved to ever meet or create or interact with Orlando. I'll be the first to admit he can be as much devil-tormentor as teacher-beloved, so it's certainly a double-edged sword. But in all seriousness, I think he is a reflection and manifestation of who *I* am - and so it stands to reason he is going to be every bit as much a trickster as a mentor.

As far as our doubles are concerned, we create them through our actions in the Now, through dreaming, and through writing our identity on the fabric of the nothing with the quill of Intent and Will. That being the case, it doesn't have anything to do with justice or whether we deserve something or not. I suspect that whole idea of worthiness comes straight from some Catholic program that occasionally seeps out of its cathedrals and into our awareness. Either that or a Monty Python skit.

Thou art god. There is no other.

What a Long, Strange Trip it's Been

The following events all occurred within a three day period in May of 2005. Over the years, I've pondered these occurrences at length, coming to no specific conclusion, except that it is through our chance meetings with the infinite that we become more keenly aware of our existence and our purpose within the Now.

~

Even as it was happening, the whole thing reminded me of a scene from a Hollywood horror movie. We had left Carson City at dusk after what had already been a bizarre weekend, and as the Suburban rolled to a stop on the side of the road, I looked in the side mirror to see that the tire had completely separated from the rim and now lay smoking on the rocky shoulder. It occurred to me with a complete sense of detachment that this wasn't a crisis, just an inconvenience, though that conclusion began to shift considerably when neither of the cell phones had service due to the mountainous terrain; it was beginning to rain, with a threat of snow before morning; and we were quite literally in the middle of nowhere in the foothills of the Sierras.

I was considering my options, and had just made the comment to Wendy that if things got too bad, we could always eat Erin - our hippie-chick worker who travels to the shows with us and was sitting quietly in the back seat. She didn't think much of my plan - can't say I blamed her.

So there we were - no cell service, so no AAA. The car jack didn't have the right fittings to lift the trailer, and though I had asked the trailer manufacturer for a jack that *would* lift the trailer in an emergency situation, he had steadfastly assured me that it would always be easier to call AAA, because even with the jack, he had said, we probably wouldn't be able to lift the sucker without unbalancing the load, and so...

We sat in the car for awhile, hoping for a highway patrol to wander by, or a tow truck, but no one came. Just an endless line of semis out of Reno. Tried a couple of houses nearby, hoping someone could call AAA for us on a landline, but either no one was home, or no one was going to answer their door in the middle of nowhere. Can't say I blame them either.

After about 15 minutes, I looked up to see the shadowy silhouette of a man, backlit by a bare-bulb light shining through the broken window of what appeared to be a workshop attached to a small cabin that appeared either unfinished, or falling into ruin. Literally looked like something worthy of Wes Craven. Though the man was not old, not young, he was dressed in ragged pants and a dirty shirt when he came up to the window and asked if he could help. When we asked if he could call AAA for us, he said he had no phone (and again I was feeling like I was in a horror movie script), but he said he did have tools and would change the tire for us.

I didn't sense anything particularly negative about him, and so I decided to see where the universe was going with this scenario. He went back to his workshop, limping slightly as his shadow bobbed over the uneven ground, made larger than life by the harsh light. When he returned, carrying a tire iron and a shovel, it was all I could do not to chuckle at my own predicament. The voice of gnosis said, *This can go either way. Reality is what you make it.*

So while Wendy and Erin stood holding light and tools as The Man wriggled underneath the collapsed trailer with a jack perfect for the task, I stood back slightly, observing the situation, ready to assist or defend, as need be. And, slowly but surely, the old rim came off and the spare was installed... but as the trailer was lowered, there was a collective grimace when it became obvious there wasn't sufficient air in the spare even to limp to the nearest gas station - at least 20 miles behind us. The odd thing was that I had checked the spare before departing on the trip, so this also seemed an unlikely complication, but nonetheless, there it was.

"No problem," our hero told us. "If you want to pull into my yard, I can put air in the tire with my compressor."

And again I thought of Wes Craven, Freddie Kruger, Jason. Also thought of Gandhi, guardian angels, and the voice of gnosis. The man's yard was completely shrouded in trees, behind a locked gate which he had to open with two or more keys, and all but undetectable from the road. Once behind that gate, not even passersby on the highway would be able to see us. And yet, gnosis kept insisting, *This can go either way. You choose.*

So I pulled the rig into the narrow driveway and while Wendy remained in the car, Erin and I stood outside waiting for The Man to return once more from his workshop. Miraculously, in a few minutes, he re-emerged with a small, portable compressor, a length of hose, and all the proper fittings. That in itself seemed quite strange to me. Had we managed to break down in front of the house of The One Guy who not only had the skills, the strength and the ability to deal with this, but also had all the right tools, including some uncommon couplings?

So it would seem. The Man went about the task of pumping up the spare, guided me as I turned the trailer around in an extremely tight space, and then just stood in his driveway smiling as we thanked him and prepared to pull back onto the road. There was something about him, still backlit in the shadows, standing there in his shabby clothes with his faded baseball cap. He had the demeanor of the coyote - the laughing trickster - as if he knew something we didn't. It exuded from him like a tangible presence. Though we had offered to pay him, he would take no money.

"Thank you," I said again, from the driver's seat. But it didn't seem sufficient. So I decided to ask, "What's your name, by the way?"

He nodded his head. "Marv." That was all he said. But somehow, that seemed to be enough - for me, and for him. We drove out of his driveway as he closed the old rusty gate behind us, and within half an hour, we had backtracked into a nearby town in a warm, dry hotel room as it started to rain heavily and continued throughout the night.

The next morning, after getting a new tire and the spare remounted, we again headed on our way. As we came to Marv's place, we pulled up next to his gate and left a small token of our appreciation on his gate - a Celtic tapestry in warm, masculine colors - with a note expressing our appreciation.

There was no movement in the house, no signs of life at all. And perhaps not surprisingly, the place didn't look any less threatening in the daylight than it had looked the night before. What struck me was the odd sense of power, and how it had operated to bring things together in the manner they had come together. Had the tire gone flat a mile before, there would have been no shoulder at all. Had it gone flat a mile later, we would have been paralleling the Walker River, where there are no houses at all for 50 miles.

There's really no eerie conclusion to this tale - just a sense of curiosity that has continued to linger. I think of Marv from time to time, wondering who he was, or if he was ever really there at all, or if he was a manifestation of the nagual, an ally in humanform. And the words of gnosis hang in my mind, rather heavily at times: *This can go either way. Reality is what you make it.*

~

Perhaps it all started to go weird on Friday, while all the merchants, actors and encampments were still setting up for the Renaissance faire scheduled for the weekend. We had more or less completed our large merchant set-up, and had gone wandering around talking to friends. I was still puttering around when Wendy returned with a somewhat confused look, and informed me that a good friend of ours had just started yelling at her. At first I laughed, figuring it was one of Wendy's pranks. But when she insisted it was quite real, and that she really had no idea what had happened, I decided to wander over to Sue's place and ask what was going on.

I've known this woman for years. She's a seamstress with a good reputation and a kindly demeanor. So I approached her as I always have, only to have her suddenly turn on me like a wild woman, grey hair pitching and tossing in the brisk wind, face red with anger, eyes blazing fury. The only thing missing were fangs and a red velvet cape, for she literally flew at me like some legendary creature of the night, screaming in my face about I-don't-know-what.

My detachment surprised even me, because there was a time when I would have leapt into the fiery furnace just from the perception of being attacked. Now, after so many years on the path, all I could really see was that Sue was out of her mind with anger, yet I also knew it had nothing to do with me in reality.

So I let her rant until I finally figured out what was going on. Turns out, she was angry to discover Wendy and I are participating in an event later on this year - a faire that is long-established, but recently raised its rates to merchants by literally 300%. Needless to say, it's a financial hardship on all of us, but it is also the best event we do all year, and to boycott it would be slitting my own throat. Unbeknownst to myself, Sue had started a boycott of the event, and when she found we were not supporting her efforts, her immediate response was to fly into this mad rage-dance, hurling accusations and even threats at such a shrill pitch, it didn't take long before a crowd started to gather.

I felt for her pain, but I also knew I couldn't support her cause. Causes are only masks, obfuscations. I tried explaining rationally why it might make more sense for her to simply bite the bullet and do the event as she has always done, but all she could see was that it was wrong for Them to do this or that. It was "an insult". It would cause a chain reaction in all other promoters, and to her way of looking at it, I was somehow responsible for the whole thing. In other words, she was taking the whole thing personally, but attempting to shift blame onto anyone willing to wear it rather than addressing the real issues of how to get around the hardship.

What I saw in this old friend was rage, but it was fueled by fear. The old cliché, cutting off one's nose to spite one's face sprang immediately to mind.

So I let her rant some more. For about 15 minutes straight, unabated. Friends standing nearby whispered in my ear, "Jeezus, Della, are you going to let her talk to you like that?" But what I knew was that she wasn't really talking to me in the first place. She was talking to herself. She was venting her fears, painting them in red on the surface of the air. Finally, when she paused to take a breath, I simply walked over to her, put my arms around her, and just held her while she started to weep uncontrollably.

Her fears had blinded her to any other options, all other possibilities. Slowly, the crowd dispersed, and Sue and I began to talk. I offered some suggestions and alternatives that might enable her to do the event. I honestly don't know if she will embrace one of those alternatives or retreat again into her fears. All I know is that as I stood there observing her rage, what I was thinking about was how "the play" has such power to trap us if we're not careful. When we start to think it matters or it's the end of our world, we become lost in the tempest of that fear, and subsequently we may blind ourselves to other alternatives, other opportunities.

Recently, someone asked me how we integrate (in their words) "all this fancy warrior bullshit" into our everyday lives. For me, I see it all the time, in the machinations of my everyday, mundane life. If I had allowed Sue's fear to draw me into her rage, a friendship would have been lost and perhaps worse. If I had allowed my own initial fear and suspicion of Marv to create reality, I have no doubt that the words of gnosis may have played out differently. *This can go either way.* Orlando has often said that we program others how to program us - not a particularly pleasant realization, but one I have found to be true. If I had reacted to Marv with outright fear, who's to say how he would have responded out there in the night with a tire iron and a shovel?

We create reality through the position of the assemblage point - and having the ability to choose that position of the AP is what this path can teach us.

The next morning we continued on down Highway 395 and into the heights of the High Sierras. The drive is particularly stunning, with Mono Lake emerging out of the mists like some alien vista worthy of a science fiction movie. We stopped briefly at the Walker River where the winds were brisk and cold, and the water was running fast, hard and muddy - a testament to the rains of the night before.

It was when we were descending from the Sierras around Lone Pine that we noticed the long line of traffic stopped up ahead. Turns out five semis had been overturned by the fierce winds, and the highway was closed to high profile vehicles. So we waited on the side of the road for over two hours. Erin got out her drum and sat in the field drumming. Wendy hiked to the front of the line to talk to the officer in charge about when the road might open. I dozed in the passenger seat.

Finally, we dragged out the map and began searching for

other alternatives, since night was rapidly approaching and we were still several hours from home. The highway patrolman had suggested returning to Lone Pine and getting a room for the night - though that sounded all too much like a repeat of the night before and the flat tire. So we made the decision to proceed east on a secondary road which would take us skirting through the edge of Death Valley and eventually lead back to the main highway beyond the point where it had been closed.

Even though paved and maintained, the road to Death Valley was clearly not well-traveled, but somehow that seemed appropriate, even comforting. No semis tearing past at 100 mph. No immortal teenagers dodging in and out of traffic. Just the three of us and the parasitic cargo trailer bouncing along behind us. It felt like a weight back there - a burden. I had the odd thought of wanting to cut it loose and watch it go crashing down some steep cliff in the heart of Death Valley - just a bunch of baubles and meaningless trinkets scattered like graffiti on the sharp rocks.

I said nothing. The scenery was magnificent - colors so intense, like nothing seen in nature. Again, I was feeling as if I were on some alien planet. At a lookout point called Father Crowley's Vista, the winds blowing up out of the canyon were so fierce they literally threatened to strip the clothes from our bodies. I've stood in a hurricane a time or two, and this made those tropical storms pale by comparison. Overhead, a flock of birds dived in and out of the stiff currents, and I realized I was standing at the crack between the worlds. The sun had slipped low on the horizon; a mountain to the west cast the world in shadows that grew longer with each passing moment.

As we descended from the higher elevations and into the valley far below, I began to notice a peculiar phenomenon for which I have no explanation. The mountains to the east were still catching the last rays of sunlight, whereas the peaks to the west were completely in shadow by this time. At the base of the western mountains, a lavender mist had settled in a long strip which extended the entire length of the range - several miles that we could see. At first, I thought it was nothing more than a trick of the light, but then Erin commented on it, and it soon became obvious that we were observing a real phenomenon. This purple mist would brighten and expand - almost like a flash-bulb - then it would return to its more normal presentation of a strip of mist at the base of the mountain. We observed this several times while passing by a hand-painted sign.

Ghost Town - 4 miles.

From time to time, a rickety old pick-up would pass us going in the opposite direction, though we couldn't help noticing that the people inside appeared out of the ordinary in one way or another. Like caricatures ripped from the page of a cheap western novel. The old miner with only three teeth and a scraggly beard, grinning from the driver's seat of a truck that hasn't been built in 50 years. A young man in a cowboy hat with a scarred face, riding in the back of a pick-up no less worn than the first one.

The nagual was in full swing, having a bit of fun with us. At least that's how it felt.

There are no explanations, of course - only Power, which sent us on the detour in the first place.

What a long, strange trip...

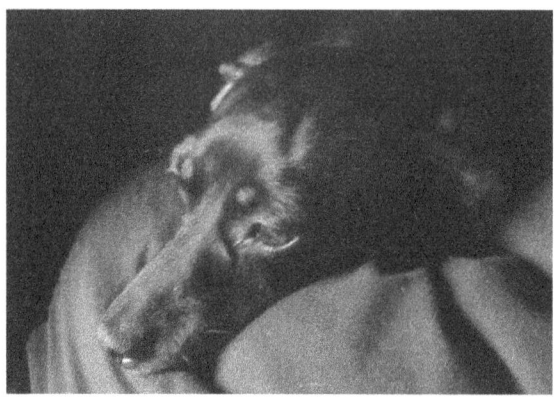

Dust[6]

The late afternoon sun was sneaking through the cracks in the mini-blinds to create a diffused world of long shadows as I woke from a nap to find my weenie dog sleeping peacefully against my chest, the cat curled up purring at my knees, and the essence of a sapling eucalyptus drifting in through the open window. From the kitchen, the scent of spaghetti sauce brewing in the crockpot filtered into the mix, and the sound of my lover moving around in the next room gave a sense of utter well-being to my world.

Less than a second had passed since waking as I took a slow, deep breath, marveling at the way the setting sun was playing with all the strange and dusty trinkets on my old altar - no longer used much, but nonetheless a standing icon to the days when ritual was used to hone and focus Intent.

Dust.

A pain stabbed at my heart - not in any physical manner, but in Spirit. And I literally felt the little smile that had been tugging at my lips fade back into the world of Dreaming. Something in the dust had brought me back to ordinary awareness, to the Knowledge that whispered in the voice of tree leaves dragging softly across the window, *You are a being who is going to die.*

In an instant, I had been transported forward or sideways in the belly of Time, and the dust on my altar had become the ashes of the being who had inhabited the assemblage point of

---

[6] To watch a video of this entry, go to
https://www.youtube.com/watch?v=BX4jyNTrcMY

"Della". Perhaps it was 50 years in the future, or 5 months or 5 minutes. All I knew was that my time on Earth had ended, and I was standing to the side, watching, as other humans sifted through the ruins of all those things we leave behind when we leave this world. Funny, actually, that most of what we spend a lifetime creating ends up in some thrift store basement, or at the leading edge of a bonfire. The ashes of our self-importance scattered to the winds of Neverland.

It was as if I were watching the aftermath of my life play out on that old altar, where journals have gone to gather dust, and hawk feathers and raven feathers and hatched snake eggs and broken beads and melted wax and little pebbles found in rare desert streams and a gaudy plastic pirate ring from Disneyland had found a resting place for a brief time. The items themselves have no power, of course. They are only trinkets of a phantom past, souvenirs of a life. The sun seemed to caress each one, and then the room fell softly and inevitably into the darkness.

For a few moments in that stillness between the worlds, I wanted to weep. And yet, at the same time, I wanted to jump up and pound my fists against the quantumly cold chest some God who had, according to the prevailing myth of our society, created a perfect world and then in his anger, imbued it with Death. It matters not in the least that there is no such being to whom we may turn our anger and our frustration. What matters it the absolute and undeniable realization that we are beings who are going to die.

Something in that equation has always struck me as ironic and utterly inefficient; and despite the Knowledge I have gained on this path, that sense of wrongness has not changed. In fact, it's partially what motivates us as warriors - the sense that we are in a prison awaiting our own death sentence, and the only way out is the path to freedom that enables us to shed the organic body and trade it instead for the energetic vessel of the double.

It also matters not in the least that I have gained an absolute understanding of why things are the way they are. Without Death and Love and the two-part migration of the soul, chances are we would be little more than idyllic bliss ninnies running about the garden sipping honey from the bees and frolicking naked beneath The World Tree with our genitals flapping in the wind. It is clearly the existence of Death that gives us our motivation to run for our lives through the jungle of all existence, carving a path toward our own evolution with a blade of pure Intent that has a tendency to slice away some of that beautiful foliage of the garden. Sometimes, it seems we can pause barely long enough to enjoy that One Perfect Moment of long shadows and sleeping weenie dogs and the dust of time on the journals of our journey.

Sometimes I have to wonder, without expectation of an answer, if this is simply the way things are, or if something went horribly wrong in the matrix that has resulted in this strange state of affairs wherein we find and even embody those moments of perfection, only to be forced to release them just as quickly, as Time grinds forward like some ruthless predator devouring our youth and whispering that the dust on the altar is really the dust of old friends and pets who lie sleeping in the ground, and our own future history writing its name in itself, in the dust of the Now.

Sometimes, knowing that I am a being who is going to die

makes those perfect moment all the more perfect. Other times, it makes them all the more perfectly painful, and that is what drives me to run outside in the night as an eleven-year old girl, and shake my fist at the sky, and howl in despair and intent, "If I can't come to you, I'll bring you to me!" The double answered that little girl's cry, of course, and yet...

The dust on the altar defines a warrior's melancholy.

Death, Immortality and the Sorcerer's Trick

As much as we have discussed in various online forums and chat rooms and coffee shops that the life/death conundrum is part of a natural cycle, I remain unconvinced. Visions I have had consistently over the years have spoken of what amounts to a flaw in the matrix - the flaw being that we are made of temporal organic goo that breaks down all too quickly, instead of the starstuff of the Infinite and Eternal.

The universe is not normally so inefficient with energy, so why now? Granted, we have the ability to overcome that flaw through our creation of an inorganic body of energy (the double), yet the flaw itself remains. The program of Life crashes just when it gets up to speed.

I have wondered if the so-called "end of time" has something to do with that flaw being corrected on a universal scale. Might even tie into my own ongoing riddle: "You have to *be* immortal before you will know how to *become* immortal." If we were immortal, Time would cease to exist.. We create Time, and in doing so, we become its mortal prisoners.

I know my comments fly in the face of our most deep-rooted program - the belief that says "all things die". And yet, if we don't challenge our most intrinsic programs, if we don't at least ask the question, we may be missing opportunities that cannot exist until we open the door of possibility.

So, I'm wondering if the actual point isn't being overlooked. As warriors and seekers we go through life challenging all our programs, stalking ourselves with ruthless intent, dismantling belief systems, and hopefully emerging with a shifted assemblage point that allows us to *see* the world and its illusions for what they are.

Why is it, then, that most warriors seem unwilling or unable to challenge The GrandPooBah Program of *All* Programs: the idea that "all things die"? Is it simply that the program is *that* deeply ingrained in us, or is it that we fear even looking at the equation of our own finite existence? Are we in denial as individuals, or only as a species? Can one determined monkey engineer a paradigm shift by proving the earth really isn't flat, or is the desire of the other monkeys to go on living on that flat earth so overwhelming that the one monkey has no power over the matrix at all? *Do* all things die, or do we only *believe* this because the program tells us it is so?

I am not certain in the least that the program is accurate or inaccurate. It may indeed turn out that all things die, or it may turn out that only some things die as a result of going through the motions of Death actually occurring. So, I am merely suggesting that for as long as we accept it as an established fact we are living on a flat earth because we have accepted that the earth really is flat.

Is it?

For as long as we believe we are beings who are going to die, we live our lives in a manner that validates and creates the foundation of that belief system. Who knows - maybe we really are just mortal sacks of flesh and bone, but how would we even know if an immortal were sitting elbow-to-elbow with us in a dark movie theater? There are certainly legends and rumors of beings who have shifted into an energy body without the dubious bother of actually passing through death.

What machination of Intent and Will would be involved in making that transcendent leap with our awareness wholly intact, without actually dying? Is this what is meant by "burning with the fire from within" - going from our mortal body bag to a vessel of pure energy as a matter of Will?

What I'm getting at here is that the biggest program of all seems to be the one we accept almost without question. All things die.

I'm not so sure about that. Are you? Are you *really*?

When Wendy and I initially began this journey with Orlando in November of 1994, he allowed us to believe it was a quest for immortality. Being human, we interpreted that as meaning physical immortality, simply a continuity of life in the existing body-form. He did nothing to correct that idea, and in fact encouraged it for quite some time - and with good reason. If he had said, "No way, physical immortality is impossible," chances are we would have turned away and gone looking elsewhere, because our mindset was such that we would not have accepted other alternatives at that time.

So, being a master stalker with infinite patience, Orlando allowed us to believe what we needed to believe while, at the same time, he was teaching us about eternal beings, infinite awareness, energetic structures existing as inorganic awareness, vague references to "the twin" (now more commonly called the double), and so on. He simply couched it in different terms so as to maintain the foundation he had with us.

Over the years, we began to realize the seeming impracticalities of a physical-form immortal - namely that it would be highly at risk if the earth were to be smashed by a wayward comet or if the humans decide to wipe themselves with some designer virus or several well-placed nukes.

Also, over time, I began to actually *see* the connection between Orlando and myself, and finally - around 1998 or so - I clearly *saw* that he is my double, who had been in the process of "dreaming me" ("teaching me" works just as well) for several years at that point. What all of this boiled down to was a paradigm shift that caused me to realize that my teacher/mentor was *mySelf*, and in order for that to Be, it meant I would have to deal with the concept of an energy body as the vessel for my immortality, since Orlando was clearly something altogether other than a humanform man. Therefore, on some level, it had to mean that I myself was more than just a handful of chemicals and some water.

The process of assimilation on all of that took many twists and turns, and what it all came down to was the realization that we cultivate our awareness and cohesion in the here and now, but we store it in the energy vessel of the double so that it transcends the state of "death".

We create our own immortality through the double.

> *"It is true there are immortals among you who have transcended the organic form without ever having passed through the portal which you call Death. There are also eternal beings surrounding you in Infinity and Eternity - singularities of consciousness who have lived and died a thousand times within the span of a moment that can only be called Now. I can tie on flesh that would appear altogether organic to you, but it is a garment of starstuff and snowflakes and blue equations that have no finite solution.*
>
> *What is Death? It is the muse and the mystery and the madness that chases all humans from the cradle to the grave. And yet, if you are truthful with your Self beyond all limitations, you will see that you do not need it anymore than you need feathers on your wings.*
>
> *When a sorcerer learns the trick, the trick is knowing that you have the power to transcend into Infinity from either side of the portal. To the warrior who has become a woman of Knowledge, we are inorganic beings without boundaries or limitations. The sorcerer's trick is creating her twin on the far side of the abyss, without fear of making the leap which removes all doubt and terminates all separation. That leap may be made through the portal of death, or altogether on this side of it.*
>
> *Orlando: January 15, 2006*

———

Once Upon an Eagle

Once upon an eagle there was time, and so once upon a time there was an eagle. He wondered how he had come to be an eagle, for he could not see his reflection in a mirror - largely because there were no mirrors in the land where he found himself as a tiny speck of awareness one day. Was it day? It must have been, for the sun was shining brightly in his eyes. Bright, so bright. Surely all things must come from the sun and return to it, for its splendor was beyond question. Yes, that was the answer. All life came from the light and returned to it, where it would begin again. It was as good an explanation as any, and so he chose to Believe it with all his heart, even though it was really only the sun.

Since there were no other theories, the eagle decided that 1) he was an eagle; and 2) the light at the end of the tunnel of darkness from whence he had come was the giver and taker of all life.

For awhile - who's to say how long? - the eagle roamed the void looking for others like himself, but because he could not see his own reflection, he could not really know what he was looking for. When he came upon a frog sitting quietly at the edge of the dark sea of awareness, the eagle was ecstatic and embraced the frog with such fierce affection that the frog was obliterated instantly, before the eagle could ask his questions. The eagle was devastated, because the frog was quite a beautiful little thing, yet now the eagle could see that he was not like the frog, and that he had made a terrible mistake.

Not knowing what else to do, he took the frog into his mouth and swallowed it whole - so that he might understand it better and honor its death by giving it continuity within his own body, which he could see now was quite different from the frog. *Why does it take death to show me this?* the eagle wondered. *It must be that all things die, and only by drinking the awareness of what it was to be a frog will I ever understand what it is to be myself.*

That was his next belief – which, although it had no basis in actual events, made a good story for Eagle to tell himself in his increasing despair.

And so Eagle continued his journey through the world, looking for others like himself, but encountering only a plethora of lifeforms who ultimately bore no resemblance whatsoever. The eagle perceived himself to be alone, and in his loneliness, he became angry and vindictive. Trying to hold the hummingbird in his hand, she died, fluttering wings going still, until the eagle could only devour her tiny little body in an effort to consume the unique essence which had been She-Who-Floats-In-Air.

When the eagle encountered the coyote, and thought once again that he had found another like himself, he was dismayed to discover that Brother Coyote had no wings, and liked to whisper in strange tongues about secrets and mysteries which only other coyotes would understand. *Other* coyotes. The eagle heard these words and was outraged. The coyote had kindred families. The coyote was not alone in the void. And so the eagle - having learned his strengths - embraced all the rabbits and ground rats and field mice in Mr. Coyote's territory, until coyote himself was consumed by the eagle's wrath and starved to death in the desert.

Death.

Though the eagle had come to see that all things were filled with Life until he embraced them, it was only when all the world became permeated with the stench of death and the awareness of the eagle's power that he began to catch glimpses of himself in the dying eyes of all those beings he had embraced. In coyote's glazing eyes, the eagle saw that his own eyes were not so different. He concluded, therefore, that he must simply be another form of coyote with feathers instead of fur, with wings instead of forelegs. Surely that was the answer - but because coyote was dead, the eagle could not ask him what he saw. In the eyes of Sister Rabbit, eagle saw fear, and recognized it in himself, though he was loathe to admit it. So Eagle wondered then if he were prey, just another insignificant creature running for its life in the miasma of Chaos Incarnate.

Eagle continued his search far and wide, but found nothing like himself in all the lands both terran and spreading to the far reaches of the farthest galaxies. Eagle was alone. And he wept for that, and in his grief and his anger, he hid behind the bright light - knowing its beauty would draw all things to it in the end, where he would be waiting. Waiting. Hungry. Angry. Alone. And all things came to him, as he had hoped. The essence of the baboon sought the light at its death, and the eagle was fed, though still hungry, for the baboon did not contain Eagle's answers. The sparrow came as well, and was received by the hungry eagle as a morsel that might tell him something about himself, but ultimately told him nothing. The sparrow was not himself. There was no reflection. There was no resonance. There was no love.

Love.

Eagle had heard the word carried on the lips of many beings. The hawk had spoken of love when he fell from the sky, leaving his mate to mourn his passing from desolate snow-laden treetops with a cry that would go forevermore unheard by the beloved for whom it was intended. Baby squirrel had whispered of love when plucked from his mother's breast – but Eagle did not know of this thing, this "*love*", and so he devoured the baby squirrel anyway, ignoring the mama squirrel's cries of grief.

In his despair for what he did Not-Know, Eagle wept with such a mournful wail that the world was split by the sound into day and night – the darkness and the light. Eagle himself determined that he would walk the crack between the worlds, for he seemed to be at home in neither place, and no matter how many creatures he consumed, there were no answers for him. He did not die, yet he could not seem to live as the other creatures lived either. He was utterly alone even though some of the 2-legged beings would smile and nod at him as they passed him on a busy street corner somewhere in the neighborhood of New York or Los Angeles or London or Rome.

"How odd," the eagle mused, "that these fragile beings pretend to know me, and even seem to like me! Do they not realize I will devour them soon enough? Any one of them may contain my answer – and if I must devour all of them to get to it, that is what I will do!"

And so Eagle went right on devouring everything in his path, then spitting it back out as its dis-integrated fragments of energy so that it could go seek some other manifestation that might bring more Knowledge to Eagle. But no matter how many creatures he consumed, it was all only a hopeless and endless stream of memories which, in the end, did not have any ability to hold themselves intact once the physical shell which had housed the creature had returned to the dust.

Then one day, for no reason Eagle could determine, he came upon a young woman sitting on a bridge at the crack between the worlds. The beautiful light had faded below the horizon. The moon mistress had not yet shown her face. The two worlds were colliding. Eagle could sense the young woman's melancholy but not the reason for it, and as he gazed upon her, he realized she did not even look the same as the other 2-leggers upon whom he had been feeding for eons. Whereas most of the others were luminous reflections of the Great Light, this one was like a black egg which held her light and her secrets to herself. So because he was curious and bored and despairing, he flew down out of the self-perpetuating shadows and sat down on the bridge next to the woman's left shoulder. Far below, the dark sea of awareness glistened, reflecting starlight and the face of the young woman, but not the eagle. After all this once upon a Time, he still could not find his own reflection.

Though she clearly knew he was there, the young woman did not turn her eyes upon Eagle. Instead, she gazed into the depths of the sea of awareness, saying nothing. Tilting his head, Eagle glanced at the woman, then at the dark sea, then at the woman again. He could not explain what he saw, but it was clear to him that her silence came from the dark sea and would return to it. This perplexed Eagle, causing him to speak before he even realized he had a voice.

"You do not seek the light," he said to the woman. "You sit here at the edge of this vast and foreboding sea of awareness, and turn you back on the light? Why is this?"

The woman did not turn toward him, though legend says she may have smiled just a little. "My reflection is not in the light or the darkness."

Eagle did not understand her words, but something in him stirred. A deeper sadness interrupted his lonesome journey. "I have no reflection," he said, mostly to himself. And the sadness magnified tenfold as he looked at this woman on the bridge between the worlds. It occurred to him to simply devour her and be done with it – for she was a disruption to his well-ordered routines – and yet there was something about her that caused him to hesitate.

As if sensing that hesitation, the woman laughed, swinging her legs back and forth as they dangled over the side of the bridge. She seemed so young, Eagle thought, yet she was clearly a wise old crone behind the eyes. She seemed so unafraid and completely unconcerned.

"Silly bird, you're looking in all the wrong places for your answers. You're believing one thing now and another thing tomorrow, and in your dissatisfaction with your *Self*, you destroy everything that crosses your path instead of looking to see that your reflection is right in front of you." The fact that she said these things to Eagle – *He-Who-Destroys-All* – without any shred of fear or respect caused his shiny feathers to ruffle for a moment.

He leaned forward, ominously, close to the young woman's throat. But she didn't withdraw or shriek or throw herself at his mercy, as so many had done over the centuries.

She just went right on gazing into the dark sea, and that outraged him all the more.

"Do you not know to whom you are speaking?" Eagle demanded. "Do you not know who I am, what I will eventually do to you?"

The young woman sighed softly and, to Eagle's surprise, reached out to caress his feathers in a gesture that caused him to tremble and weep. Then, for the first time, she turned her head and looked him straight in the eye – something no other living creature had ever done.

"I know who you are," the warrior woman told him with a certainty that rendered him altogether spellbound, for it was a confidence and a stability that went beyond fear of him and instead told him that he was accepted. He was loved.

But then she shattered his world. "I know *exactly* who you are," she repeated, looking deeply into Eagle's stillwater eyes. "Do *you*?"

Because Eagle could not answer that question, he knew he could not destroy this peculiar young woman sitting on the bridge at the crack between the worlds. So when she got up and continued her journey toward the distant stars rather than the blinding light, Eagle could only gaze after her in wonder and awe and an odd feeling of familiarity.

"Who am I?" he called after her.

She did not turn to look at him, but held out her left arm and gave a soft, loving whistle. "Come on, pretty bird," she said as the stars were coming into view. "I'll show you. In the end, you may not like the answer anymore than I do, but the journey itself will be phenomenal."

"But I am alone!" Eagle protested. "It is my nature to be alone, to devour all things, to be feared."

The woman never looked back, just laughed softly into the gathering dusk. "You're not alone. You're unique. The reason you can't find others like yourself is because we are the only One."

Eagle was spellbound. His attention was hooked. Seeing

the woman retreating, he knew he would be left behind if he waited. And so, he hesitated for only a moment. Casting a look over his shoulder toward the dark sea of awareness, and another in the direction of his fading past, he spread his wings and went to land on the warrior woman's left shoulder, where he felt a most unusual sense of familiarity, as if he had been there all along.

And though he still did not know precisely who he was – for the warrior woman was clever enough to stalk her mirror with impeccable intent and unconditional love - he had a most peculiar feeling that he was much closer to an answer, much closer to seeing the reflection he had been searching for since he first discovered himself as a tiny speck of awareness. Soon, Eagle thought, he would see himself in the warrior woman's eyes. Soon.

It was a new beginning somewhere at the edge of once upon a Time.

Stalking the Eagle

Once Upon An Eagle was one of those things that seemed to write itself, coming fast and furious through gnosis, almost quicker than I could get it all down. When all was said and done, the eagle is the self. The force that creates us and potentially obliterates us is the same - the will of the warrior at the level of *I-Am*.

In that regard, death is equal to all other things, and yet it's the warrior's ability to say *I-Am* even on the far side of that bridge that determines the ultimate test of impeccability and cohesion.

The eagle is just the motivating force - comprised of exactly the same fears, hopes, dreams, loneliness, happiness, cunning and love that comprise the warrior herself.

Even warriors sometimes try to put the eagle outside of themselves, but the danger is when the warrior forgets that the reflection sitting on her left shoulder has been with her all along. And so it seems the eagle is stalking us in the guise of death, when the actuality is that the eagle is our self-created demon (angel? god? alter-ego?) who motivates us to embrace our tightest cohesion and look into the eyes of our own infinite reflection.

For several years now, I've Known that the eagle is part of the self, perhaps made to appear extant at times for reasons we may not wholly understand, or perhaps it is both *us* and our reflection, the infinite shadow we cast as a result of standing in front of that Great Light.

I also personally subscribe to the notion that the eagle is a vast and incomprehensible Duality within the nagual - it is both internal and extant, simultaneously. It is both personal to each individual warrior, yet completely detached from all warriors. It is both unique to the self, yet it would not know you if you greeted it with a smile. It is the *I-Am* and the creator of the warrior, yet it is also the obliteration of our awareness if we do not gather a cohesion that is sufficiently greater than the eagle who is monitoring our journey and simultaneously participating in that journey.

You were born inside what you might see as the matrix, the physical illusion which is the culmination of billions of years of physical evolution. Evolution is the act of willing your consciousness to inhabit eternity as the Wholeness of all the previous evolutions. Total awareness, assembled simultaneously into past and future, now and then, eternity and infinity. That totality, if it can maintain its cohesion beyond this mortal timestream, beyond the eagle is the cohesion of I-Am.

I am the eagle.

You are the eagle.

The eagle is the black gravity that consumes awareness because it is within its nature to do so. That is its function, just as it is the function of the sun to govern the weather and the moon to govern the tides. The eagle regulates awareness, and only that awareness which has achieved a sufficient level of cohesion can withstand the force of the eagle's gravity. Put another way, the eagle is the creator of the illusion, and it is the illusion itself. Only those who can realize that the gravity itself is also illusion will be able to break free of it. Otherwise, those that cannot break free are obliterated. That obliteration is death.

-Orlando, 2002

We create our demons so we may overcome them. We cast our shadows so we may tilt at them. We sever our wings so we may learn to fly without them.

We are a strange bunch.

Visions of the Eagle

September 3, 2004

Within the past 24 hours, I've seen too much of death. Yesterday morning on the way to LA, I observed a pickup going out of control at high speed on the I-10. Less than 50 yards in front of me, it spun out and slammed into the center divider. The thought occurred to me that if I had been going any faster, it would have plowed into the side of our vehicle instead, and at the speed it was going, there is little doubt in my mind it would have killed Wendy, who was in the passenger seat at the time. The men inside did not appear to be hurt, but they were badly shaken, and may have sustained injuries I could not determine. Though we wanted to stop to help, it was impossible, so all we could do was phone in to 911. Had we stopped, it would have endangered even *more* lives, because the flow of traffic at that point was well over 80 MPH. As we passed by them and I looked over to determine their status, it was like looking into the eyes of death - those two men thought they were dead, and it's a wonder they weren't, considering that traffic was extremely heavy.

    Before leaving to go on that little adventure yesterday morning, I had to give our vet instructions to euthanize one of our oldest cats. He had been quite healthy the day before - eating, walking around, playful - yet when I found him later in the morning, he was all but comatose, the victim of an apparent stroke. The vet could do nothing to help him.

    Finally, this afternoon, I learned of the death of two 9-year-old girls in a backyard drowning accident not far from here. The tragic thing is that I had met both of them more than once in the course of our business, since their mother worked regularly at one of the events we attend, and the girls were often there. Apparently, the girls were playing around the backyard pool, and somehow got tangled in a pool cover.

    Not surprisingly, perhaps, on the trip to LA yesterday, I kept seeing images of an eagle. "Golden Eagle" on the side of a semi truck. "The Eagle's Haven" - a sign for a church somewhere along the way. There were several others - like little signs. Dark omens.

    Death is stalking all of us.

―――

Wings, Wind and Summer's End

September 1, 2004

Lit the candle lanterns in the cactus garden tonight and sat outside underneath the stars for a long time. The wind has turned soft, and though still warm with the breath of summer, the oppressive desert heat has finally begun to dissipate. Autumn peeks in at the corners of reality, still too far away to touch.

As I sat in my lawn chair with the weenie dogs bounding playfully inside the boundaries of the little picket fence, and the older dog crashed out on her side in the warm sand, there was a single moment when it seemed everything had simply stopped. There was no time. No tomorrow. No yesterday. There was only that one eternal moment, isolated like a single cell underneath a microscope, and a sense of Knowing this was how it would always be.

What it boiled down to was that it was like a single frame in a movie, preserved for all of eternity. The universe will eventually collapse back in on itself, then expand again, and if quantum theories have any accuracy whatsoever, everything that is in the now, will be again. And again. And again. The moment of stillness was almost like passing oneself in that corridor between expansion and collapse - as if the Self I am in the now, and the selves I have been in all those otherworlds were waving at one another across the abyss, eternal participants in some infinite dance of energy over which they have no control whatsoever.

The universe seemed to have a secret. It chuckled quietly to itself, and threw falling stars the way a flower girl tosses rose petals in the path of the bride. And yet, there was a melancholy, too, for what I was seeing was a dark wedding between the mortal self and the eternal other. And though that is obviously the goal of the warrior, there is nonetheless a sadness in recognizing that this mortal coil is finite, gathered up out of the dust, and to the dust destined to return.

On one level, I understand that and accept it as the transmigration of the soul from the mortal coil into the eternal energy double. And yet, there is a tiny voice inside me that continues to cry out, "Why? Why is it like *this*, when it could be like *that* instead? Why do we travel the universe in these fragile human bodies when we could just as easily be made of photons of light or subatomic particles of dark matter? Why is it the ultimate irony that life is so beautiful, when it is seemingly destined by our organic nature to end in death?"

Water gurgling in the little pond-fountain sputtered, caught in a gust of wind.

This is the path of the Spirit, the gnostic voice tells me, with an utter sense of peace and acceptance. *The cocoon knows only that it is a cocoon, and wants only to go on being a cocoon. Only after it spreads its wings does it realize that the whole point of the journey is learning to fly.*

Upon leaving the garden to return to the house, I left a single candle burning in the archway that leads from here to there, from the known and into the unknown.

So I go on, learning to fly, feeling at times all too heavy. My wings are made of starsilk and winter-wind, candle breath and moon veins.

———

Hauntings

August 24, 2004

This house is old and large - a sprawling testament to the old miner who built her back in 1955 - and with all its natural gemstone walls and its location in the desert, I've come to expect a certain amount of oddities and manifestations of the bizarre, particularly since there are several rooms which are seldom used.

Though it is warm outside today, the interior of the house

remains cool and unusually silent, with the cats sleeping in various nooks and crannies while I go about the business of attempting to organize our business for its next outing. The light has turned more gold than its typically summer-bright-white, and the wind is tossing the locust tree to and fro, scratching at the eaves, moaning and whispering through the ducts. Chimes chatter in the cactus garden outside my window, and the cobwebs lift and float on unseen currents.

A few minutes ago, I went from one end of the house to the other, followed by Zero, who has made it her habit to be always at my heels. As I passed through the living room, I experienced a sensation in the pit of the stomach which I've come to recognize as some precursor of a manifestation from the nagual. Immediately upon acknowledging the sensation, Zero gave a short, low bark, her signal that something is afoot that she hasn't yet identified.

Coming to a sense of greater awareness, I entered the room where I had been headed, at which point Zero began to bark fiercely (well, as fierce as a 7-pound weenie dog can get), and I turned to see her hackles raised. Her teeth were bared, and she was staring fixedly at a point just to my left. Aside from the wind playing with the curtains and causing them to flutter, I saw nothing - until suddenly there was what I can only describe as an energetic "flutter" in the empty space about three feet from me. There is no correlation other than in the special effects of movies - a shimmering of the air, perhaps most accurately compared to heat monkeys dancing on hot pavement in the dead of summer.

For a few moments, I stared at this anomaly with a combination of curiosity and mild disbelief, while Zero continued to bark and the fat black cat scampered past me and out the door.

Then, abruptly, it was gone. The dog stopped barking, the wind paused in its eternal journey, and whatever had been there was simply not there any longer.

After a few moments of silent contemplation of the event,

I began walking back through the house, only to hear an uncharacteristic stirring through the ducts. Having lived in this house for many years, I am familiar with all the voices of the wind, all the whisperings of the timbers, all the noises an old house in the desert might make. This was none of those. Instead, it had the sound and the feel of someone weeping softly to themselves - a hushed but profound sobbing which went on for at least 30-45 seconds. And then it, too, simply stopped.

A sense of melancholy lingers in the house - not unlike the paradoxically exhilarating sadness one feels when autumn begins to slowly creep up out of her dormant sleep. The nagual shimmers and weeps, haunting this old house in a way that has raised gooseflesh on the back of my neck, and leaves me with an ache in my spirit that has no explanation.

---

42 Minutes

Over the course of my life, I've had many unusual experiences, but perhaps none so strange as an incident that occurred back around ~1995, wherein I woke in the middle of the night (3:38 a.m. to be precise), and walked from one end of our old rambling house to the other, went into the bathroom in my office, then came back out and returned to the bedroom, only to discover that I had been gone for approximately 42 minutes. The clock which had read 3:38 a.m. when I left the room now read 4:20. I could account for perhaps 2-3 minutes. But certainly not the 42 minute interval that had ensued.

In the grand tradition of humans, I tried to convince myself I had simply looked at the clock wrong, until Wendy rather sleepily asked me why I had been gone so long. So to *her* perceptions, time had passed, whereas to my perceptions, I had been gone less than 5 minutes.

This has been an incident I've pondered often over the years, and through a couple of attempts at regression, I have been able to extract certain images of what might have occurred during that interval of missing time. Over the years since then, there have been at least a couple of other incidents of a similar nature - I would look at the clock, walk across the room, for example, then look at the clock again, and 42 minutes would be missing. Again, I could account for perhaps 3 minutes, so a pattern was beginning to develop - intervals of almost exactly 42 minutes of missing time, occurring somewhat regularly. Not in any exact pattern I can discern, but at least once or twice a year *that I was aware of*, and who knows how many times that I simply haven't noticed.

Then, just 2 nights ago, it happened again, with 100% certainty that I didn't simply glance at the clock wrong. Woke up in the middle of the night, glanced at the clock. 4:44 a.m. Got up, looked out the window at the cloudy night (a beautiful rarity in the desert), took note of the fact that dawn was just beginning to break behind the clouds, then returned to bed. Again, I could account for approximately 2-4 minutes, and yet as I was climbing back into bed, I glanced at the clock. 5:29 a.m.

At first, I again tried convincing myself I had simply glanced at the clock wrong. How adamantly we try to explain away the mysteries of life! But as I looked at the windows, I realized it was *much* lighter than it had been when I gazed out the window in the bathroom. The horizon was now pure silver, the pre-dawn brightness which can be almost blinding at times. No doubt that approximately 42 minutes had indeed passed, for it was validated by the difference in light.

So what is the significance of 42 minutes? There is absolutely no sense of a glitch in my personal timeline. No sense of having dozed off, no sense of having passed out, no evidence that *anything* is out of the ordinary, except that 42 minutes is missing from my life, and that this significant interval of missing time continues to occur occasionally, without rhyme or reason that I can detect.

Is this some function of heightened awareness? And, if so, why 42 minutes? Is it a biorhythm? A tick of the cosmic clock? And how often does it occur that I *don't* notice, simply because I don't happen to be aware of time. Not wearing a watch and not being a clock-watcher, I can't even begin to imagine.

I fully realize that missing time is a function of the so-called UFO experience, but that doesn't track with my own perceptions and my own awareness. Just as Carlos Castaneda had absolutely no awareness of events taking place in heightened awareness until years later, I suspect this could be part of that same process.

There is simply no way to know, and that, too, is part of the journey.

———

Death and Dying: "Somewhere"

October 5, 2006

Just before going to bed last night, the little voice of gnosis said, *Leave your cell phone in the living room.*

Because of my mother's terminal illness, I had been keeping the phone next to the bed for months, so when that little voice whispered its instruction, a strange sense of destiny came over me and a weight I had not realized I'd been carrying seemed to lift from my shoulders.

I went to bed around 11 p.m. and slept soundly until 6:25 in the morning. At that time, I was awakened by a presence I recognized to be my mother. Though I did not see her, I knew she was there, and through a telepathic channel, she gave a little laugh and said, "Well... I went *somewhere*." There was no sadness or fear, only a sense of amusement on her part.

"Do you know where?" I asked.

Again that familiar laugh. "It ain't here," she replied. Before I could say anything else, I felt her embrace me. "I love you." A brief pause, then... "Bye."

And then, always a woman of few words, she was gone.

I sat in the pre-dawn darkness for several minutes, contemplating the peculiar but reassuring exchange, then got up and went out to the living room where the answering machine was flashing frantically and my cell phone had recorded over half a dozen missed calls. I sat at my desk for a moment and smiled, remembering something my mother had said when I was just a little girl. *'When I die, I don't want nobody getting a phone call in the middle of the night. I'll still be dead in the morning.'*

Upon talking to the nursing home, I learned that she had stopped breathing at 3:38 a.m. - a moment in time which has special significance in my own life, as previously discussed. It is also significant that day my mother passed would have been my father's birthday as well.

There are no coincidences, only ironies which validate the nagual.

Long before the sun came up, I went out walking in the desert alone, watching the world coming back to life. Two mourning doves flew overhead. Cottontails stood like frozen silhouettes against the pale sand. The sky had turned a brilliant shade of fire.

"I went... *somewhere*."

Her words left me with a smile, a sense of mystery, and a feeling of peace. There is no better gift she could have given

me.
    Peaceful Dreams...

Letters to the Double, Written on the Wind

February 27, 2007
    There is a certain sound the wind makes in the night. I cannot call it a voice or even a whisper, just a murmuring of some ancient memory that stirs me awake from a fitful fevered sleep, to find myself sitting up in bed, legs crossed, head tilted forward, pillow clutched to my chest, and the scent of you sketched on the cold air of the darkness as if you were standing in some otherrealm of the multiverse, in some reality where we were just children on the beach together, then sweethearts, then an old married couple rocking together on a wooden porch held together by the gossamer filaments of a love that transcends all reason in order to become the reason itself.
    Sometimes you have even encouraged me to play with such thoughts, and in fact I recall you once scolded me for daring to call them 'fantasies'. "Everything begins with a thought," you said, and I heard the words as if for the first time. "Think of me as a fantasy and that is all I will ever be. Dream me with the force of your unreasonable longing, and I cannot help but be everything you want me to be, for that is the nature of energy in motion, the manifestation of creation through the relentless application of Intent."
    I remember the night long ago when we had that conversation, and now it comes again, still riding on the broomstick of the wind, returning to my haunted room at a time when I need to hear it most. Nothing is impossible except what we determine to be impossible, and even then the determination itself is only a thought which may be

eliminated with another thought that whispers in your voice, *All things are possible.*

I wonder at times where it is all heading, and why the journey seems so fast, just a drop of mortal blood on the vast canvas of the infinite. But even as that thought finds its way to the surface again, I can almost see you like some illumined doorway set against the shadows - an outline of light in the shape of a man through which the entire scope of all things may be accessed. The stars are only grains of finite dust against that mind-boggling tapestry, and all things that can be imagined only a thimble-full of wine in the bottomless cup of all possibility.

The wind stills, gusts again, and seems to be laughing. The scent of you presses closer. The totality of myself embraces me, and I hear my heartbeat like a fluttering of tiny wings somewhere in the night that never ends.

"By allowing the impossible, you discover what is real," you tell me, like a lover whispering secrets.

So said the wind in the middle of the night. And so it shall be.

Old Photographs

March 22, 2007

Finally arrived at our destination in late last night - spent most of the day today going through the house and essentially filling trash bags. Found myself thinking throughout the day of the odd futility of life, yet the strange irony as well. Not so long ago, my mother was a living, breathing entity, in love with this little house in Central Florida, happy to just be able to walk in her yard and rake at the oak leaves. Now, somewhere in the next county, I am told her urn was put in the ground back in October, yet her presence lingers here in the house as if she never really left.

Ironically, I can't help thinking that one day someone will sift through the rubble of my life and inject 99% of it into garbage bags, and that's okay, too. I had expected to feel sad during this process of undoing the remains of a life, but instead there is only a sense of amused irony. We walk the earth for awhile, gather a few trinkets, only to have it all scattered again when the spirit and the flesh file for divorce one day. Funny, that.

Both Wendy and I find ourselves gravitating outside to the yard - 2.5 acres of live oaks that form an overhead canopy of green. I hear the breath of the nagual again, and it reminds me of a childhood I left behind, yet never really left at all. The little girl me is still out there somewhere. The spirit of her is still chasing fireflies and leaping over fallen logs, pursuing the edge of a dream that never really ends.

No matter. In a single day, we have emptied more than half of the house - funny, since it took my mother more than five years to fill it. One thing I found odd was discovering so many old photographs - relatives whom I never met, most without any notation as to who the person was or where the image was captured. Just haunted faces in stalwart black and white, peering through the tunnel of time from Then into Now.

At first, I found myself gathering some of the photos into a large box, but then at the same time I would hear the voice of the nagual whisper, *Why? Time for it to end. Time to break the cycle that has no meaning left to it.*

I understood that more than I wanted to, perhaps. I wondered how long my mother had been carrying those photographs around, and if even she would have been able to say who those haunted faces belonged to. There is no doubt that all of them are ghosts now, all that remains just a dog-eared bit of photo paper and sometimes a faded date stamp.

There was something strangely freeing about finally tossing those old photographs into another black trash bag and setting them in the yard to be hauled away to the dump. One day, sooner than I might like to think, someone will do the same with all the old photographs I have gathered over the years. Perhaps they will look at the woman in the picture and wonder who she was... Or not.

Either way, it was an interesting reminder that we are all little more than bleached photos in the pages of time. What lasts cannot be held in a plastic trash bag. What doesn't... is already dust.

———

Voices From the Rubble

March 22, 2007

I remarked to Wendy yesterday that there are no manuals for how to deal with the aftermath of a close relative's death. Or if there are, they are probably written by stuffy men with letters after their name, an attempt at healing broken hearts by old farts who never had a heart in the first place. While it isn't my intent to be irreverent (too late), I have found that sifting through the rubble of my mother's life has been more of a trial than I might have thought it ever could be.

The old clothes that no thrift shop would want. The broken furniture that probably came from a thrift store in the first place. The hoarded plastic margarine cups dating back to 1975. The lingering scent of cheap perfume stored on the back shelf of an old woman's cupboards. The cat bowl, left by the fridge, empty save for crumbs.

As a warrior, it is within me to be utterly ruthless and without attachment when necessary. Those are not just words. That is my life and how I have chosen to live it, and so even though there is a sense of melancholy that accompanies the death of anyone who has been loved, there is no real grief in the way most humans tend to think of it. For me, that has been as it must be, for there is a soul-deep understanding that we cannot even begin to wrap our minds around what lies beyond our ordinary awareness.

So we sorted through most of the household stuff, bagged up what could not be salvaged, gave away what anyone wanted, and consigned the rest to a large pile in the front yard. This morning, an hour before dawn, the dump truck arrived and was left parked in the yard for us to fill. It was a task I had not looked forward to, because even as a warrior it is impossible not to see the irony of life as well as the mystery and the beauty of it. The things we have gathered over the course of a lifetime are cast away in a few minutes by those left behind, and that, too, is as it must be.

And yet...

While Wendy was still sleeping and I was alone in the midst of the rubble, before the sun had come up, before the wind had begun to stir, before the horizon had even the faintest hint of color to it, I began loading the trash bags into the dump truck almost by rote, pondering the briefness of life, wondering if there is any meaning to any of it.

So for a moment or two, I found myself irrationally angry and then sad and then angry again at the whole concept of death. Though my mother and I were never close in the way many mothers and daughters are, I could certainly acknowledge that she was a good woman who got the short end of the stick in many aspects of her life. I could argue that with myself and say her own choices led to her circumstances, but I could also see the other side of the coin, which was simply that she was an old woman before her time, perhaps not really capable of making "better" choices in the same way a younger person might.

But as I was tossing 50 pound garbage bags full of socks and underwear and old photographs into the dump truck, it occurred to me that the world was slowly but inevitably breathing itself back to life. The eastern horizon had lightened to a dull, cold silver. Birds had begun to sing. An old pick-up lumbered down the street with one headlight pointing up at the trees, the other poked out like a wounded blind eye.

It all seemed so strange. Just fucking *strange*. No other word for it, really. Like a bit of celluloid running through an old projector, occasionally hanging up in the gears and fluttering in and out of focus.

The house next door was coming to life. An old woman with strikingly white hair moved tentatively out into the garden, where she began watering a row of corn. Another neighbor was heading out to work. The Croomacoochee wild oaks were filling the air with a golden pollen that floated on the wind like finely powdered snow.

For a few moments, standing in the back of a dump truck amidst the remains of my mother's earthly belongings, all was right with the world. A part of me that grew up nearby felt comforted, at peace. I would keep the property here if I could, yet on the heels of that thought comes the very real realization that it is not my destiny nor my choice to be here. This part of the world is like a window to my past now, which I may gaze through from time to time, but do not really want to become a doorway through which I might be tempted to walk for reasons too numerous to mention.

As I stood there watching the sky turn brighter, I continued tossing the trash bags into the truck, barely noticing the breaking of glass that seemed like an echo of finality, a statement of closure. A pitcher that had been around since before I was born shattered. Old water glasses, well-stained with Florida rust, tinkled like wind chimes. An ancient music box that had not played in years suddenly chirped out several notes of *Fur Elise* from somewhere in the rubble.

And then I heard the voice. "Three thirty eight a. m.," it announced. "Three thirty eight a.m."

A woman's voice, soft and melodic. At first, I could not imagine what it was, but as I kicked at a bag to get it out of the way, the voice came again. "Eight thirty five a.m.. Eight thirty five a.m." Another kick, and, "Nine twenty seven a.m. Nine twenty seven a.m."

Only then did I realize it was a talking clock that had been next to my mother's bed for several years. Touch the button in the middle of the night, and it would whisper the time. But when I kicked the bag, it once again repeated, "Three thirty eight a.m. Three thirty eight a.m."

So I stood there and did not move for a very long time. According to the nurse in attendance at the time, my mother stopped breathing at 3:38 a.m.

Do I believe in coincidences? Not really. Do I think it was my mother's way to yelling at me for breaking that old pitcher? Doubtful - she always hated the damn thing even though she liked to pretend otherwise.

So of all the possibilities for that clock to choose - 24 hours in every day, 60 minutes in every hour - it just seemed like a calling card from the nagual in amongst the rubble, like a jester passing through the edge of a death dream to murmur something of significance, and then simply disappear.

The dump truck is loaded. The yard and house are empty. The music box has sung its last song from the heart of the ruins. The clock has fallen silent.

Our work here is almost done.

———

Assembling Magic

September 1, 2007

When I was little, maybe up to about age 5, my Crazy Granny was my guardian during the day, what with my mother at work and my father absent even when present. I remember at least three or four times sitting on top of an open door. You know - the door is open into a room, and there I would be sitting on the *top* of it, sort of swinging back and forth with Granny shaking her cane and telling me, "Now you come down from there the same way you got up there and don't you ever do that again! People will talk!"

What's funny is that I didn't *get* up there, at least not to my perceptions. I simply decided to *be* up there, and there I *was*. And I'm pretty sure Crazy Granny knew that about me, which was why she insisted on taking me to church every Sunday and engaging in the old practice of beating the devil out of me. Yes, look it up. People of her generation actually believed that children needed a good beating on a regular basis to  keep the devil at bay. God is love. Om and what the hell? Funny beliefs.

I once heard her talking to my mother when neither of them knew I was around, telling her how I was a sprite. "People will talk." That was Granny's worse fear, of course. Didn't want all those god-fearing Christians down at the First Baptist Church thinking she was in league with Satan's little minion.

As I say, I barely remember these incidents now, and yet even still I sometimes look at an open door and have to laugh. It was so easy to just *be* there.

Something else of a similar nature was that I would find myself outside at night - down by the swamp or just sitting in the back yard underneath one of the long-needled pine trees. I never felt any sense of fear or duress, and I know the incidents were physical because on nights when they happened, I would wake the next morning with all manner of dirt and debris in the bed.

Finally, I also have a bizarre experience which I refer to as a "memory that never happened." I have a very distinct memory of walking down a road in the middle of the night - a road that was very familiar to me, where both my school and the church were located, directly across the street from one another. In this memory, I have a complete awareness of who I am, and again there is no fear even though in ordinary awareness this is not something I *ever* would have done. The awareness that accompanies this memory is that I had been to a meeting of some sort - something that had occurred in one of the out buildings of the church. There was nothing sinister about it, but it was very secret and in terms I did not possess at the time, I would now say it was something that occurred in heightened awareness. What I remember most is walking down the road toward home, having to duck behind a tree at one point when a car approached.

A few years back, Whitley Strieber published a book in his *Communion* series entitled *The Secret School*, which resonated with me at a very deep level and prompted other similar memories from that same time period in my life. While I'm not particularly in alignment with the "alien visitors" scenario Whitley presents, I do believe that something profound happened to him, and his mind processes it in terms of "visitors" whereas others might process in terms of heightened awareness. No matter. For anyone who has had similar experiences, this book was a good catalyst, recommended reading.

There's something very magical about those times for many of us, I suspect. What's also of interest to me is that as I have progressed on this path, I find that these quasi-memories of the other self become more accessible - as if working with awareness in the now also affects awareness of things that occurred in the past.

And yet, with so many years in between, how can we go back to that childhood innocence that enabled us to do the impossible?

How can we tap into that aspect of the self in the Now? I don't think we lose the ability, but instead we lose the assemblage point from which that ability functions. So as with most things on this path, it becomes a matter of shifting our awareness to a place where it is simply *natural* to use those abilities. As a child, my assemblage point was certainly not where it is now, so I think it would be a matter of moving the AP to that place on the energy body in the same way firewalkers shift the AP to a position which tells them, "Fire does not burn." When we inhabit the energy body as a position of the assemblage point, those abilities which were so natural and easy as children are once again accessible in the Now.

Sometimes I honestly think we are so human that we need validation from other humans in some things. Our programming is such that if you tell me you can fly, I am required by society to tell you that you are nuts and call the proper authorities while making the appropriate harrumphing noises of disbelief. That's what my Crazy Granny spent her lifetime doing - denying what was right in front of her because her programming told her it was impossible or demonic or whatever.

So how do we take this to the next level? I think part of the work we do is to validate to one another that we're *not* crazy, and that these phenomenal things *do* occur. For many, that's more than half the battle! Carlos Castaneda once said that we validate this non-ordinary awareness through special consensus - so in a way that's what seekers are to each other. A special consensus.

Beyond that, it becomes a matter of experimenting with movements of the assemblage point.

When we agree to allow the impossible, we begin to tap into those other abilities which are so troublesome to Crazy Grannies and Baptist ministers.

———

The Dream House (Part One)

January 5, 2000

Woke up at midnight in a state of absolute panic, though I can't say whether it was something internal or something extant. My mind immediately began running lists – *Is your heart beating? Are you breathing? Is the house on fire? Is someone trying to break in?* I never figured out the cause, though it took several minutes before I was able to calm down enough to go back to sleep. Then woke up shortly after 3 a.m. feeling very paranoid – bumps and thumps I don't normally associate with the house settling, and a general feeling that someone was in the house. A little voice in my head was yammering two contradictory messages: *Don't sing it into being!* and, *Don't ignore this feeling that something is wrong!* Wendy was awake and I tried explaining it to her, only to discover she was feeling paranoid, too.

We waited. Nothing. Waited. Still nothing.

Finally we went back to sleep. It was sometime after 7:15 that I dreamed of being in a huge white house on the sea. In the dream, I am inside the house, looking out a huge plate glass window that faces the ocean. To the right, I see a peninsula of land that juts out far into the sea, and on the left is a much shorter outcropping of land, perhaps nothing more than a large rock abutment.

When I see this scene, it is very deep dusk, and the moon hangs low on the horizon – so this would have to be a waning moon probably very late in the year.

The setting is very precise, and there is a deck approximately ten feet wide completely surrounding the house – wood planks, natural in color. There is also a wood railing, actually a half-wall of wooden boards at the edge of the deck, and at certain places there are built-in benches with red or red-orange cushions.

My dream more or less ends there. Wendy then wakes up and begins telling me of a dream she'd had about Orlando, her own double, and another young man. As the details unfolded, I realized we were in this exact same house I had just dreamt. Within the context of her own dream, Wendy was compelled to tell me it wasn't a dream. In fact, in her dream, Orlando was adamant that she realize, *"This is not a dream. This is real."*

As we sit in bed discussing our shared memories, it's as if I can remember Wendy's dream. I can see Orlando standing on the deck in the clothes she describes – not because she describes it to me, but because I was *there*.

While meditating on this later in the day, I caught a flash of understanding which told me we store these heightened awareness memories "elsewhere" – whether elsewhere in the brain, or elsewhere within the realm of non-local information. Wherever it is, it's not the normal brain-loation we access when looking for memories of what we had for dinner last night.

The Dream House (Part Two)

July 30, 2001

Just returned from a long weekend in San Diego at Imperial Beach Sandcastle Days. While there, we discovered the dream house.

On Saturday morning, as I walked to the end of the street and turned the corner, it was to find myself standing directly in front of the house from my dream. At first, my rational mind tried to explain it away. Certainly there would be discrepancies. Surely it was only *similar* to the house in our dream.

And yet, as I walked toward it and began studying it, every detail was exactly as I had dreamt it. The rock jetty and the peninsula of land on the right as one stands and faces the sea. The pier on the left. The sand birm between the house and the beach. The terraced decks and lounge chairs just to the side of the house. The long, relatively narrow back porch, all closed in glass. All of it, exactly as if plucked from the dream.

What amazes me about this is that if any aspect of our journey had been different, we never would have found it. For example, when we arrived at the show, our original booth location was a block further south – and if we had remained there, I would have taken a different route to the shore, a different street, and I never would have seen the house. If we had cancelled the weekend, as we considered doing, we would have left the area without ever going down to the shore. Everything had to come together in a very precise order for us to ever see the house at all.

In *The Eagle's Gift,* Carlos Castaneda talks a lot about "memories that never happened" – experiences which occurred in heightened awareness, which he only starts to remember when he is with La Gorda and the two of them are dreaming together. At some point, he also discusses the idea that these memories that never happened are stored in a different memory center of the brain, not normally accessible during ordinary awareness - the same conclusion I reached independently. And yet, as Carlos progressed on his journey, it became obvious that he was beginning to access those "quasi-memories of the other self" with his first attention awareness.

There is something critical to this – this ability to begin to "remember the other self". Perhaps that is what it means to actually awaken from the dream – to literally step into that larger world and inhabit the heightened awareness, become the immortal "other self" rather than returning automatically to this illusion we think of as our mortal life.

Perhaps that is the definition of evolution – when we enable ourselves to be whole instead of fragmented into beings of our ordinary awareness and beings of dreaming awareness, locked apart from one another through limited perception. As much as I would like to think otherwise, I do not feel this is an automatic accomplishment that comes to us at death. Instead, if we achieve it at all, it will be because we pushed ourselves to expand beyond our traditional human awareness and into the other-than-human evolution.

I feel like Dorothy, having just opened the door into Oz. The question now becomes: how do I find the wizard and capture the reflection of my higher self in my own shiny mirror? How do I stay in Oz instead of returning automatically to the drab gray fields of Kansas?

Light on the Lake

September 30, 2007

It was a certain way the light hit the lake, the way the sun bounced off the little chops on the surface of the water. No way to describe it, really. A hundred different elements had all come into play with just the right timing. A pale silver mist, not quite fog, not quite cloud. Scent of cut grass. Hint of mystery on the wind.

Just words, meaning nothing.

What seemed to matter was the fact that it caused my breath to catch in my throat. I was 17 again. Back on the shore of some half-remembered lake in Florida when I was still just a girl, chasing bullfrogs and courting the infinite without having a name for it.

It was an afternoon when I had cut school with one of the local boys. Doug, I think his name was. We snuck off to a lake that had no name, floated out to the center of the water on a cheap raft, and spent the day talking about whatever it is that teenage kids talk about.

What I remember about that day back then was looking toward the shore and noticing how the trees grew almost to the water's edge. The shadows. Thick and black and inviting - far more inviting, even, than the embrace of the handsome young man in whose arms I was lying. He was known somehow. No mystery. The shadows and the orange groves and the black bottom lake were the mystery, calling forth something in me that I had never felt before in quite that manner, until that afternoon on the lake.

I knew then, somehow, that I would never be completely content. No man would ever be enough. No friend would ever know me as I wanted to be known. And yet...

There was something in the shadows that knew me. There was something in the trees that was kindred.

And for a moment today, I found myself back in that assemblage point, overwhelmed with that sense of wonder and awe and melancholy perfection which simply cannot be spoken of except in 3 a.m. campfire whispers. For a moment, the world stopped, and I was neither Della the girl, nor Della the woman. I was simply - *somehow* - the synapse of energy between the two assemblage points. I was the manifestation of the nagual, reaching across the void to *be* the shadows which have drawn me to this moment, to *become* the light on the lake, reflecting back and forth between then and now and then and the infinite.

For that moment, I knew my name... written in a language of light on the lake, and the shadows that lie between this world and the next.

―――

The Twins

September 23, 2012

I encounter twin girls who appear to be 9 to 10 years old, strawberry blonde hair, and dressed in cotton flower-print dresses of a style that was popular in the late 1950s.

In my lucid dreaming state, I am remembering a technique learned from Orlando years ago. It is acknowledged that 99.9% of those we encounter in dreams are just projections of our own awareness – false echoes. Very rarely do we encounter actual extant beings. One way to determine if a character you meet in a dream is real is to ask their name. If they are false echoes, generally they will either vanish altogether, or will take on the qualities of a zombie. Most often (there are exceptions, of course), phantoms will not be able to tell you their name in a dream.

So I said to the little girls, "You look identical. Are you twins?"

They nodded in unison.

I then asked, "What are your names?"

The girl on my right met my eyes with an intensity that

was astonishing. "My name is Time," she said.

The girl on my left had an equally penetrating gaze as she revealed, "My name is Death."

Then, in unison, they said, "We are identical."

I cannot express the intensity of their being.

I was instantly awake, pondering Time and Death in the dark on the first night of autumn.

I feel certain I will meet the twins again.

The little voice of silent knowing says to me, *Don't let their appearance fool you. Don't let their innocence trick you.*

Indeed.

———

A Machiavellian Dreaming

January 4, 2002

A very odd and disturbing dream last night. Basically, I was a warrior returning to my homeland after a long and difficult period of war. I was male, Orlando in the flesh. Wendy was with me, though she, too, had inhabited her double and was a tall blond male with long hair tied back in a series of long braids. We were walking side by side through a lush and beautiful landscape, probably somewhere in 11th or 12th century Europe.

We were approaching a very large building of a somewhat Spanish-style architecture - red tile roof, adobe-like walls, with several sets of huge double doors made of wood all around the building. Could have been a church at one time. The back story of the dream was that we were warriors of an army that had been defeated, and though this was our homeland, it had been occupied by a new ruler. The new king had stated that it was his intent to absorb the defeated warriors into his own army because we had been clever enough and strong enough to survive, and were therefore the best of the best of our people.

I said to Wendy as we approached this building, "Here we be, soldiers returning home from war, and it is the intent of the new king to kill us on our home soil." Wendy was shocked at this, having believed the king would truly keep his promise to integrate the surviving soldiers into his army as a gesture of solidarity between the new ruler and the conquered people.

"Why would he do that?" she asked me, though in a dialect of Olde English. I looked at her, but *saw* her as the male warrior with whom I had been friends and companions for an eternity. In that moment, we were Alexander and +Hephastion and a thousand other pairings throughout history. We had simply manifested in a form that was familiar to the mind of the dreamer.

In response to her question, I said, "Because that's what I would do. We are the ones who fought the hardest battle and lived to tell the tale. He cannot afford to have us alive."

And yet, it was known to me that to *not* to go this ceremony would put us in defiance of the king, and we would be killed anyway. And so, it was one of those impossible situations. We entered the building, where a multitude was assembled - hundreds of people. We sat near an exit, and I recall saying to my beloved friend, "If pandemonium breaks out, go for the exit." We were not armed, yet the soldiers of the king's loyal army carried heavy swords and weaponry. I overheard one of them say to another, "If they break for the doors, they will be most surprised to find our finest swordsmen on the roof."

In short, I had a feeling we were done for, and all in some political maneuvering scheme that was used to force the surviving warriors to essentially enter the building like lambs going meekly to slaughter.

A most frustrating dream, particularly for the symbolism. I have a feeling in retrospect that we were warriors fighting in opposition to one of the Crusades. Don't know whatever happened, for the dream fizzled out at that point, though it has haunted me with possibilities as to what it meant. I have seldom dreamed of being in the past or the future. If I believed in past lives (which I don't), I would suspect this was something of that nature. Instead, I'm inclined to think it was the warrior's eternal struggle, recognizing the traps, realizing that the greatest enemies are often those posing as allies.

A Simpler Life

September 22, 2004

As I was writing the article you are about to read about "a simpler life", I heard a loud *smack!* against my office window - a sound I have come to recognize as that of a bird wiping out. So, in the midst of everything I have to do in order to get ready to leave tomorrow morning for our next business outing, I went outside and picked up the poor critter, and just sat on the lawn chair for awhile holding him in order to assess the damage. At first, I thought he would certainly die - mouth open, gasping, non-responsive.

The thought occurred to me that perhaps I should simply place him at the base of one of our large trees and let him die in peace. For certainly, I thought, he must perceive me as some gigantic predator come to eat him whole, for he was only a tiny little sparrow. Pretty little thing - primarily brown, with some dull yellow markings at the tips of some of his feathers, and yellow veins running down his flight feathers.

It also occurred to me, *I don't have time for this.*

That thought grabbed my attention. I took a look at my morning routines, considering all the things I needed to do. Load the truck. Load the van. Hook up the trailer. Tidy up the house. Go to three different stores. The list was endless, while I sat immobile on my lawn chair holding this injured bird. There really wasn't anything I could do for the poor critter, I thought. Holding him in one hand, palm flat, he was still limp and dazed, but at least he had opened his eyes and was looking at me. I didn't see any blood. He hadn't moved. But suddenly he let out a loud squawk. *Fear*, I thought, but I talked to him gently nonetheless.

So me and the bird sat there for several minutes while the world went right on by at its crazy pace and all those things I needed to do were left undone. By now, the little fellow had wiggled his wings a bit, and was trying to regain the function of the percher-muscles in his tiny little feet. I had some major trepidation about one leg - for he couldn't seem to unfold his foot at all. Again the thought came to me that I should assist him into a tree, and then leave him to find his fate. After all, I thought, if I hadn't interfered in the first place, he probably would have died of shock on the ground underneath the window; or else he would have just lain there and recovered... or been eaten by a road runner.

I had interrupted his journey.

By this time, he's squawked a few more times and stretched out his wings. That one leg is still a problem, but suddenly he flies out of my hand and goes to land in a sapling I just planted over the summer - a scraggly white birch that's also been struggling for life. They seemed like perfect companions, except the bird was hanging upside down like a bat, obviously unable to use that one leg to perch properly. By the time I got to the tree, he had fallen out and was lying on the ground with his delicate underbelly exposed, and I had the thought that we were both wasting our time.

But I picked him up anyway and took him back to the lawn chair, and sat there with him for a few minutes longer. Finally, he flew again, with the same disastrous results, though now he landed in a chaparral bush and flopped upside down in a tangle of brambles at the base. The trailer is sitting there unloaded, a few feet away. Seeing the car reminds me I have to take it in this morning, because the air conditioner was making a weird racket yesterday. Nothing is getting done, and this bird seems hell-bent and determined to die anyway. And I can hear Orlando laughing somewhere in the background of the infinite, asking, *What difference does one little bird make in the grand scheme of things?*

Orlando, of all inorganic allies, knows perfectly well that the bird makes no difference, yet *all* the difference.

Being a stubborn bitch, I wriggled underneath the chaparral bush, dug through the brambles, and picked the little bastard up for what I had said to myself would be, "the last time." He's squawking and protesting, still having trouble with that leg, but at least he's got a fighter's heart and is telling me he wants to live. So we walked a short ways together, and then he suddenly flew out of my hands and made it to a more distant tree. Hung upside down like a bat for a bit, flopped on the ground, fluttered like a leaf in the wind, then finally picked himself up and flew to another tree.

There, he landed right-side up on a branch, shot me a dirty look, and made a motion that was probably the sparrow-equivalent of The Bird Finger with his bad leg.

I felt a lot better about the whole "waste of time".

―――――

Shadow Play

Home at last after 11 days on the road for the Lake Tahoe Renaissance Faire. After two flat tires on the way up, a malfunctioning car alarm that seemed to be caused by a ghost in the machine, and a satellite dish torn clean off the roof of the motor home (yes, I *did* check the overhead clearance, but the rope blended in with the scenery), we are finally back home.

One very peculiar incident however, which occurred in the little town of Bishop. I was driving the motor home, Wendy following behind in the Suburban. I had been fighting fierce winds for over 100 miles already, so severe at times that my nerves were on edge and my temper beginning to heat. It was literally like being slapped around by an unseen opponent, and the thought crossed my mind that it was also like sparring with Death. No matter how good a warrior might be, Death will always have the advantage just by virtue of being relentless, immortal and having no need to sleep.

As we descended into the foothills of the Sierras, leaving behind the magnificent beauty of Mono Lake and Mammoth, I was watching the wind pitch and bend a long row of cottonwood trees that line the road on the approach to Bishop. The wind was so strong that it occurred to me the trees might snap as leaves were torn from their branches and sand pelted the side of the vehicle like a hard rain.

To my surprise, as I was looking at the treetops, I heard Orlando's voice through gnosis, as he laughed a little and said, *Ah, but look at the shadows on the road.*

As I did, a strange chill passed through me despite the warmth of the day. Though the treetops were being pitched and tossed like so much kindling in a hurricane, the shadows on the road were dead still, as if the shadow and the thing casting the shadow were existing at two separate points in the space-time continuum. That's how my mind instantly translated it. The shadows, it seemed, were from some other place and time.

Stopped at a light, I could only gaze in amazement at the swirling treetops blowing in an angry tempest contrasted against the shadows on the road that may as well have been painted there and left to dry in the warm, dry wind blowing in off the nagual.

Stopping the World

The day itself was an entity, a personality shrouded in grey and drifting clouds, misting rain that was cold but oddly unwet, and a pervading darkness that caused one to believe it was dusk even in the early afternoon of the Los Angeles pre-Christmas madhouse.

Though I did not particularly want to be there, there was a part of me that was secretly in love with the bleak nature of the storm and the face it had painted over the tall skyscrapers and crumbling gothic-style hotels that stand side by side in a landscape of dichotomous duality which occasionally looks more like a flat matte painting than anything remotely real.

I wandered alone while Wendy was busy in one of the shops. Familiar territory, but grim and cold now, streets flooded, and an odd scent permeating the damp air - the stench of human urine, street-vendor hot dogs and stale perfume wafting out from one of the nearby wholesale outlets.

The wind was cold against my cheeks, colder still against my bare shoulders and chest. I had intentionally dressed for summer, knowing it would force me to experience the rain on my flesh - a sensation which can be discussed in words, but can only be experienced in the do-ing. A miasma of language swirled around me. Spanish. Korean. Chinese. Farsi. I thought of *Blade Runner*, and the futuristic world depicted in the film.

A pang of some unidentified emotion swept over me. For a moment, I remembered being at the premiere of *Blade Runner*. Sitting maybe two rows behind Harrison Ford, watching the movie unfold around those who had created it... and the dreams I had carried with me at the time. Dreams that I might write movies myself. Fantasies that I would wear a slinky black dress and sip cocktails with Ridley Scott while chatting about artistic trends in the realm of film noir.

The dystopian future of Los Angeles depicted in Blade Runner isn't so different from how it actually appears today.
Blade Runner, Photo Copyright Warner Bros. Pictures

I had been a writer back then. And yet, there came a day when I was talking to Wendy and I said with all the truth and passion in my heart, "I don't want to be the one writing the books. I want to be the character in the book - the one on the grand adventure, hero or villain, both and neither, I want to be *doing* what writers only dream about on paper! I want to be the ghost hunter or the starship captain! I want to sit in that *Blade Runner* bar where nobody speaks English and the rain is freezing and wet against my face, and I want to feel all of that pain and the glory of the pain and the simple joy that there is anything at all to really feel in this crazy world!"

So I stopped for a moment on that rainy Los Angeles street, and realized yet again that I had gotten my wish. The power of my own intent had manifested it. Even if not in the way I might have fantasized or imagined, it had nonetheless brought me to that one moment when I could stand at the crossroads of the past and the future, looking with wide-eyed wonder. The buildings where *Blade Runner* had been filmed were barely two blocks away, and the sheer irony of it all caused me to wonder yet again how real any of it is, and how much is only the Dream within the Dreamer's dreaming.

As I stood there surrounded by the madness of Christmas shoppers literally arguing over who would get the last Baby Betty or how much they were willing to pay for some cheap statuette of the Blessed Virgin, the world simply went away. The writers went on strike. The dialog turned to silence. The actors stopped in mid-stride, and for a split second I began to wonder if I had stepped onto the set of *The Day the Earth Stood Still*.

The world... *stopped*.

"It'll be over soon, won't it?"

The voice came from my right, and as I turned my head, it was to see a paper-thin man in a rickety wheelchair, backed up into the shadowy recesses of a doorway to an abandoned storefront. As I met his eyes - haunted and full of sickness for which no cure existed, racked with the pain of his illness which went untreated as a result of his inability to pay for the continuity of his own life - I realized that he *saw* it, too. He *saw* that the world had stopped. He *saw* that the matrix had paused to take a breath.

Though there were many ways I could have chosen to interpret his question, I knew through my own *seeing* precisely what he meant. Though he knew he was dying and probably would not survive until Christmas, his question came from a position of the assemblage point that had nothing to do with himself. When he said, "It'll be over soon," it wasn't even a question.

I nodded without speaking, following his gaze upward to where a diminutive Asian man stood in a third floor window - broken and dusty - sipping coffee and gazing down at the chaos in the filthy streets below.

"You know who he is?" the old fellow in the wheelchair asked.

"I have no idea."

"That's God," the man told me. Then he laughed, though it came out as a cough. "Problem is - he don't know how to fix it either. So he just paces back and forth in front of that window all day, drinking his goddamn coffee." Another chuckle, another fit of coughing, then: "Fuck the son of a bitch. Who needs him?"

When I glanced back up at the window, God was gone. The world kick-started itself as if on the last breath of its own intent. Rain that had been paused in the air resumed its love affair with gravity, and began falling steadily. A baby screamed. And somehow I simply knew it was the birth-cry of all the world.

The old fellow in the wheelchair had gone back to staring at his mismatched shoes, the gathering droplets of rain on his silver hair like diamonds on the crown of a fallen, forgotten king.

I touched his shoulder gently, though he never looked up.

"It'll be over soon," I told him, validating what he already knew.

He had fallen asleep there in the rain, in the shadows of the grey city, in a doorway, in December.

And for that one single moment outside of time, we had Dreamed together of a storm and a broken window, and God.

The Tightrope Between the Worlds

I am not particularly sentimental as these things go, yet as Wendy and I embarked on our first show of the season - a Celtic music festival in Calaveras County, California - I found myself experiencing a variety of emotional responses which I would consider unusual.

Driving through the central California valleys, which are endless expanses of farmlands, I couldn't help noticing a certain melancholy that had soaked into the very fabric of the space-time continuum. Though the sun was shining brightly and the day was neither too hot nor too cold, there was a dullness to the photo-finish of the scenery that had little to do with my own inner equilibrium. It felt as if the land itself was feeling its mortality - an odd thought, since I have always considered the land as somewhat eternal. Blades of grass or clumps of grapes may come and go, but the earth and the stones and the water and the milieu have never really struck me as temporal, even though all things are at a certain level.

In many ways, the scenery was like a moving picture cast on the glass of the car's window. The almond trees were an iridescent, glowing green with their new leaves barely formed after a long and dormant winter, yet despite the fresh spring growth, the trees themselves exuded a sense of antiquity that was not comforting, but monotonous somehow, like a CD flickering over the same line of lyrics over and over.

Cycles of life and death, dormancy and growth, birth and decay. The trees seemed to want children to climb their branches, yet no children came to play, no sound of laughter or tears or two little girls whispering secrets in the shady grove. Just the sameness. The bursting leaves that would turn darker with maturity, then fall away in the autumn, repeating, repeating, with only a raven's occasional visit to break the monotony.

Broken down houses lined the freeway, inhabited by people with broken spirits, shells devoid of dreams. I could not feel sorry for them, for there is no doubt in my mind that all human beings have the same opportunity to become a man or woman of Knowledge. Perhaps what troubled me about them was that I knew they are no different from myself.

Every moment is filled with choices, and in looking back on my own life, I can see those crossroads moments strewn behind me like disconnected scenes in a movie. If I'd turned left instead of right, I would be a lost soul instead of a warrior. If I'd stayed home from school that morning in January of 1973, my life would have ended. If I had never cried out to the night sky when I was just a girl, maybe Orlando never would have answered, and I would be just a broken down prop in my own sad drama in a farmhouse somewhere in the middle of all that sameness.

Another thing that troubled me was how tidy it all seemed. Neat rows of well-groomed trees, broken only by neat rows of freshly-budding grapevines or rows of strawberry plants or mustard greens or little green onions. Children rode rusty tricycles down dusty roads where no shadows were cast by the late afternoon sun. There was no tall grass for the monsters to hide in, no gnarly old tree in which to build a tree house or carve one's initials as a statement of one's existence. Just little green onions in little green rows.

The world of matter and men in full spring bloom.

Later in the weekend, after arriving at our destination in the gold country of north-central California, I found myself sitting underneath a tree listening to a Celtic band by the name of Tempest as my gaze wandered over rolling green hillsides in the distance, where a variety of live oaks and pines dotted the terrain with patches of darker green upon green.

Mist swirled and danced as the daylight began to recede behind a cloud bank, and a chilly wind tossed the wild pasture grass to and fro with a lonesome whistling and rustling. The breath caught in my throat as a thick curtain of heavy dew brushed my cheek. *To be alive,* the gnostic voice whispered. *This is what it is to be alive, kissed by the cold, damp lips of eternity.*

For the first time since leaving on our journey, I began to feel at peace again. On one of those distant hillsides, a Belgian horse trotted and frolicked with unseen spirits, whinnying into the approaching storm. A hawk soaring on high currents cried softly into the thickening twilight. The music of the band had turned dark and melancholy, a sad song about tombstones crumbling in the palm of Time while ghosts play poker alongside winding, endless roads. The fact that there were no lyrics to the song was entirely irrelevant. The nagual writes its own words only to exist in defiance of them.

All of those moments have passed now, the sameness and the sadness, the sun and the shadows, the days and the nights. And yet, somewhere in the hologram, that *is* eternity - the manifestation of the infinite into the now, just a collection of images held together by the glue of Spirit which experiences them.

Such is the tightrope strung taut between the worlds.

Meeting the Brujo[7]

Circa ~2003

It began as a meditation. I often sit on the bed at night and gaze out through the open door. Since we live on a five acre parcel in the desert, I have a magnificent view of distant mountains covered by snow, and a closer vista of Joshua trees, piñon pines and yucca plants. The desert is not the barren wasteland so many envision. Instead, it is full of life in all its many manifestations.

So I sat on the bed and leaned back, enjoying the last vestiges of light splashed along the horizon. It had rained in the morning, and the scent of wet chaparral lay heavy in the air. A cold breeze was blowing in. The sky was a pale shade of winter night.

I drifted. And then I slept. Just sitting there at the edge of the desert, on the edge of the nagual. Last thing I recalled, I had glanced at the clock to see that it was 5:45. Quite some time later, I awakened to the sound of footsteps, and a man's voice. Very clearly, he said, "It's time to get up."

Opening my eyes, I discovered a naked man standing just

---

[7] This entry originally appeared in Quantum Shaman: Diary of a Nagual Woman, but since it fits the theme of *Into the Infinite* so well, it seemed appropriate to include it here as well.

inside my door, less than five feet from me. Silhouetted against the open door, there was no mistake, and yet I was completely without fear. It isn't that I am fearless. It was simply that there was nothing *to* fear, and in that state between sleep and waking, I knew this on a level of awareness that transcends all logic.

I gazed at this man for approximately five seconds - quite a long time if one is holding one's hand in flame or looking at a naked man standing next to one's bed. As I gazed at him, he began to morph much like a special effect in a movie, and as I watched with utter fascination, he turned into a large golden dog who has been frequenting our land for several weeks - a stray whom we've fed from time to time, but who has always shied away from physical contact.

In the shaman's world, nothing is as it seems. All things are only transient manifestations of energy. After the man had become the dog, I got up and went out into the yard, where he was sitting on an old grass mat, gazing at me with one upright ear and one bent ear, and a funny smile that was far more human than not. Laughing at me, I suspect. So I laughed, too.

What does it mean? Who's to say? It is known in the shaman's world that brujos can take on the shape of animals if that is their Will, so I cannot possibly know if the dog was really a sorcerer in his own right, or if a sorcerer chose to manifest as the dog. All I know is that a brujo with a sense of humor wandered naked into my house while I lay sleeping, and told me it was time to get up.

Is this some allegorical tale? Nope. Every word of it is true. Trying to wrap human comprehension around it is like trying to contain the ocean in a teacup. The experience is the journey, and the journey is the cumulative experiences that go to form a foundation of Knowledge. I was honored by a visit from a brujo, and after we played together for awhile in the open desert, he simply disappeared into the night, a shadow running along the road.

The crack between the worlds stands open. Sometimes, if

we are blessed, something from the other side slips through to remind us of our own limitless power, and the unbounded wonder that is Life.

―――

Christmas Rant

It should be noted that genuine madness may also be a manifestation of the incomprehensible. And family dramas at Christmas only reinforce that observation.

~

Circa ~2005
Every once in awhile in life, I find myself faced with a situation that genuinely vexes me despite everything I have learned and experienced on this path of Knowledge. One of those situations happens every year about this time, and can best be encapsulated with  the words, "The Family Christmas Play." Now, before I go any further, I should warn you that I am not much into Christmas these days. So if anyone is expecting a cheery holiday tale of power, you might want to stop right here and go rent *Miracle on 34th Street*. I just have a need to spew out some observations on paper and let them be whatever they are. Naughty or nice or somewhere in between.

There has been a rift in my extended family for some

years which was long ago deemed beyond resolution. Both of the primary players in the drama are perfectly okay with that, but other family members simply insist on doing The Family Christmas Play regardless of the fact that having the two primary players in the same room is rather like attempting to have matter and anti-matter in the same container without any dividers. As Mr. Spock could tell you even without a tricorder, an explosion of universal proportions is inevitable, entirely predictable, and - *note* - also entirely avoidable by not introducing the volatile elements into the same physical space at the same time. It's a no-brainer. Just. Don't. Do. It.

What is it about the holidays that makes people want to go through the motions of something that is entirely unreal 364 days a year, yet they want to *pretend* it's real on that one special day? I sit in a restaurant as a captive audience to the off-key blatherings of, *Santa Claus is Coming To Town*, and I hear myself muttering under my breath, "Would somebody shoot the fat bastard at the city limits so we can all get back to our *normal* dramas and pretenses?"

On the other hand, Christmas is a wonderful time for really observing the play in motion, because it comes to the surface far more than on any other occasion, with the possible exception of a large Baptist funeral complete with paid wailing women. In my own situation, we had been invited to the usual family gathering, with the understanding that it would be a group of five, and "the rivals" would not be present. This is the way it's been for several years now, everybody is a lot happier, there is far less stress, and if it ain't broke, don't fix it. So, we agree to the invitation, and *after* the plans are set, it is *then* revealed that the rivals have been invited. Now here's my gripe. The wording of this (a private email) is such that if we say we are uncomfortable with it, we are then ogres who must be treated accordingly. On the other hand, if we go, it is walking into a stressful pretense that couldn't be any more unpleasant than a prolonged colonoscopy.

I ask through gnosis what is the solution if I decide to go, and gnosis responds, *Just be yourself.*

And yet, to do so would come with some rather dire consequences, because if I was *myself*, I'm quite certain I would end up telling The Fam exactly *why* it is dysfunctional, why that will never change, and offering a rather untender suggestion for where they might want to put all that cheery wrapping paper.

What is it about the illusion of "one big happy family" that will make everyone go out of their way to be miserable for the entire month leading up to this "magical" day (magic has a dark side, too), when in the long run, the characters in a Looney Tunes cartoon are more real by comparison? I don't really want or need that personalized fat-gram-counter from "the rivals" anymore than they want or need a roll of toilet paper printed with the likeness of hundred dollar bills. The whole thing is nothing more than warfare concealed, and though some would say the holidays are about healing rifts and forgiving past grievances, I would say, in a single word, *bullshit*. That's just one more program running in the background - this strange guilt-and-manipulation-driven program that tries to tell you you're the original Uncle Scrooge if you don't care to suck up to family members who turned their back on you when you needed them most, and then blamed you for the entire ugly affair.

But for the sake of a few Polaroids to stick in The Family Christmas Album - if you'll look closely, you'll see Aunt Sara leaning awkwardly away from Lecherous Cousin Fred; and Brother Joe rolling his eyes just as the flash caught him; and the constipated grimace your father-in-law is trying to disguise as a smile - an entire group of people who might otherwise be happy and peaceful in their own right spend a lot of time stressing out over what to get for their estranged sister, or what to say to the uncle who molested them when they were 6, or rehearsing whatever clever line of dialog they intend to burst into the room with when the door springs open and the unseen director in everybody's head shouts, "Lights, camera, dissatisf-action!"

In my opinion as a warrior on the path for many years, this is altogether ludicrous, and once again I am compelled to remember that being unknown has a *lot* of advantages. At Christmas more than any other time, I can see why don Juan told Carlos that he had to get away from his family and friends and set out on the path of being unknown. Perhaps in some warriors, there is still a need or desire to interact with the bearers of one's DNA just for auld lang syne, but for the most part, as I observe the machinations of it all, I can only feel what can best be encapsulated with the words, "Nobody can take their eyes off a car wreck."

The world is a nut-house and the lunatics are running the asylum. I've closed more than one rant with those same words, but yet again it seems entirely appropriate here.

Some say with great feeling, "Christmas comes but once a year." To which I would reply - "Thank the merciless gods!"

Recapitulating God[8]

March 13, 2003

2 a.m. and the wind is soft and silver, a night-blanket cut from stardust and smoke from the fires in other people's chimneys. I climb the little knoll across the street and study the world as if it is a book written on the fabric of the universe - yet it is a book whose pages are forever changing in the same way dreams bend and quiver when one tries to look at them too closely. Nothing remains the same, yet everything is eternal in the Now. Perhaps that is all that can be said of the

---

[8] This entry originally appeared in Scrawls On the Walls of the Soul, but bears repeating here.

Infinite.

Gazing back in the direction of my house, I wonder if I am sleeping peacefully in my own bed, dreaming myself out here in the lonesome desert where the coyotes are prowling ever closer and the mockingbird is restless and off-key. Even the moon is a broken egg, lop-sided and bleeding albumen clouds that linger for only a moment before they are gone, like shapeless phantoms moving in and out of the night.

There was a time long ago when I wanted to believe in God.

That is the thought that comes to me, uninvited. Just the prattle of the internal dialog running its inventory of the past. And so for a moment I am 7 years old again, trying on the role playing game of belief in some old man with a long grey beard sitting on a celestial throne. But in my heart, even then, I knew there was no God, just as I knew there was no Santa, no Easter bunny, no goddess or guru who could give me the keys to heaven. There is only the Self in its many manifestations - the mortal self, the immortal Other, the eternal *I-Am* who is the cohesion of both. Just those three... my personal triumvirate. And, of course, all the identities and manifestations the Other puts on in order to learn the lessons required to teach the mortal self the process of her own evolution. A billion or so past lives that aren't really 'past' at all, but more like stories in a long book of fairy tales, with each and every character being one more Self, all of whom will turn out to be the storyteller when all is said and done.

It's enough to make my heads spin.

How very much easier it all would have been if only I *could* have believed in God. And yet, belief is not for warriors, and gods have no place in the nagual. In recapitulating our gods, we give up our faith in external sources of salvation, turning instead to a one-on-one interpersonal relationship with eternity.

A Joshua tree scratches the wind with skeletal fingers, causing the night to sing softly to itself, like an old man whistling past a graveyard where his own tombstone already stands waiting with the date of his birth inscribed, and the date of his death drawing ever closer to the marble.

Overhead, a shooting star seems to hesitate in flight, perhaps just long enough to recapitulate the fall from heaven, the destruction of faith that paves the way for evolution.

As long as god exists, you are working with a safety net. So says the Silence in the middle of a winter's night.

Alone in the darkness, we shed our gods in order to embrace the god-force of Creation within.

―――

When the Student is Not Ready, the Ally Will Appear Anyway[9]

It was approximately 1989, and I was living in a rural community outside of San Diego at the time. Had just read the first four Castaneda books and decided I was heap-powerful-medicine-warrior and that it was time to go out into the wilderness and summon an ally. (I'm lucky to be alive!) So, having picked up some vague snippet of info either from the books or an interview with Carlos, wherein it was intimated that an ally might be summoned by a rhythmic sound, I set off into the unknown.

At the end of a long dirt road was a huge metal gate, surrounded mainly by a mysterious government facility and absolutely nothing. So I got out of my car at dusk, leaned against that gate, and began tapping on it in a rhythmic fashion with my ring. At first, I felt rather foolish, but then something came over me and I decided to really put my heart into it. I projected my longing, my desire to be a warrior, my love for the infinite and the unknown. And I let myself go.

Tap-tap-tap! Tap-tap-tap!

---

[9] Originally published in Quantum Shaman: Diary of a Nagual Woman

Distantly, I heard a dog barking. In answering rhythm. *Bark-bark-bark!* Hmmm. *Tap-tap-tap-tap-tap! Bark-bark-bark-bark-bark!* And so on. Whatever rhythm I tapped, the dog would answer. I even got into some complex Jamaican drum rhythms, and so did that dog. Indeed, I was so into it that it didn't occur to me that the dog was now much closer than when I originally started my ally hunting. Nor did it occur to me that it was getting damn dark! I just kept right on tapping, and the dog kept right on barking. Until, quite abruptly, I realized I was hearing what sounded like a rustling of tall grass, the movement of wind through a rocky canyon, the rush of the eagle's wings.

Something was moving straight toward me, at a *very* rapid rate of speed. It was huge, at least twice the size of a man; for though I couldn't see it, I could sense it as it emerged from the canyon and onto the dirt road perhaps 100 feet from my car. A huge dark shape for which no words exist. I didn't see it. I *saw* it.

And I ran like hell. Jumped in the car. Fired up the engine. Spun 180. Sputtering and choking on terror, I roared out of there and went speeding toward home with "it" seeming to roll/float behind me, hot on my bumper. It was only when I got back onto the paved road that it stopped and went back, having confirmed to both of us that I was no more ready to engage the ally than I was ready to fly.

I can see why don Juan warned Carlos that the meeting with the ally could have killed him. The fright alone was sufficient to do just that.

Okay, that was really stupid. But it taught me something of incredible value. What is written of in the books of Carlos Castaneda and others is not only true for *them*, it is true for *us* if we choose that path. The impossible is possible. Magic and sorcery are real. And the allies are most definitely out there, though they are not at all what most of us think.

Since that time, I have engaged the allies by choice, but with far more sobriety and impeccability than my first foolish and faltering attempt.

Still, I must acknowledge again that I am lucky to be alive.

Initiation

In the life of almost anyone I have encountered who may be said to have "a shamanic predisposition", it seems there is a creation story to be told, and my own journey is no different in that regard. It was a few years after I had begun working directly with Orlando that the events which I will attempt to describe occurred.

While these events may appear frightening or even sinister to those outside the realms of shamanism, it's important to note that this type of initiation seems to be quite common, natural to those who have experienced it directly.

What happened to me simply *is*.

As a result, I walk in the shadows and the moonglow of the aftermath, forever changed, and with absolutely no regrets.

Since so many have asked about my "initiation", it seems appropriate to reveal the events which contributed to my assimilation of *I-Am*. And, indeed, any such initiation is a life-altering event of monumental proportions. For that reason alone, attempting to describe it with words is seldom more than an arrow shot into the dark in the hopes of hitting a moving target.

~

May 6, 1997

As I move through the underworld, guided in part by the presence of the sacred mushroom ally, it is the vessel of consciousness that enables my movement and the assemblage point of my will that directs the journey. There is no other way to explain this except to say I am drawn here because it is my Intent to be here. This is the shaman's trick. This is the sorcerer's Will.

At one point, as I find myself in an underground cave that appears to glow as if secretly illumined, I am visited by the old Native American shaman with whom I have shared Dreamings many times in the past. In one such Dreaming, many years ago, he gave me his staff as I stood at the edge of a deep gorge cut into the Earth, and so I have carried a part of him with me from that moment, and perhaps long before, even though he has never told me his name, nor asked what mine might be.

He is stern but gentle, wise but unencumbered by his Knowledge. He tells me with thoughts, never speaking, *You've had your play. Time to get to work.* Time to come into the deeper levels of the underworld. But because I'm one with the ally and time is doing strange things, I brush his insistence aside at first, basically telling him I'll get around to it before the night's done. He becomes even more insistent, and says something to the effect of, "Don't make me take off my face to get you motivated. It'll just scare you." Indeed - I'm sure it would. I hear his words and feel the energetic movement of his Intent. And yet I dally, for here Time is no master. Here, Time is no thing at all.

I get distracted for awhile, talking with Wendy. Finally, finding my deeper Intent, I say to her, "Let's just do it. Let's just go." She says my decisiveness helps her focus and that she needs a narrator to get her started, but I sense that even attempting to describe the experience is limiting it - by using the speech center of my brain, which I feel as a confined space, I am cutting off the pathways to deeper parts of the experience itself. Also, since speech is governed by time - it takes time to tell what one is seeing/experiencing - attempts to speak in anything other than broad statements seemed to drag me back into a more "linear" experience. Strange, how much we depend on language, yet how much it destroys the bigger picture. Only by going into it without language (internal dialog or external dialog) was I finally able to "do" the journey I wanted to do.

I can only describe it as a plunge into Intent - into the unknown, into the nagual. There was no journey, yet the journey was infinite, folding back on itself to its beginning, only to discover that any such sense of a beginning was only an arbitrary position of the assemblage point, where that belief in beginnings was allowed to exist. No time. No space. Just be-ing.

Just before I finally reached my destination, I was again confronted by the old Native American shaman, who asked why I was dallying in the ally when I should have been using the expanded perceptions to get some serious work done. I was *being* instead of *doing* - one active, one passive. He asks what I intend to do, and in a way that's almost impossible to communicate, I "expanded" myself to show him what I was capable of, what I could "do".

He only laughed at me, rather pathetically, because I could only "expand" to the limits of my Self - I could puff myself up like a balloon, expanding my senses, but I was still confined inside my senses, a prisoner of my self-created "self". I could only be Della; I couldn't be secrets or truths or anything else, so to keep *being* in my dilly-dally world was silly because it was so limited. In order to be more than the sum of my parts, I had to put aside that self-importance - the part of me that wanted the old shaman to be impressed. I had to evolve beyond my own limitations.

Finally, I find myself in the underworld with Orlando. In this place, there is no water that I can see, just pale sand and lots of rocks. Just words limiting the experience, but that's the hell of it. The first thing I experienced was seeing Orlando's fierce warrior-self standing slightly above me on one of the rocks. When I look up to acknowledge him, he immediately lunges down on me, baring his fangs and laying open my throat before I even know what's happening. At first, he's the beautiful humanoid *Orlando-man-animal* I've seen in visions before, similar in appearance to the man I once knew when he was in humanform manifestation, or skin-walking or whatever it is that quantum beings do when they want to communicate directly with humans. But now, in an incendiary transformation, he becomes part human, part bird, part wolf - imbued with an Intent which can only be described as unbending and fierce.

Immediately after he rips my throat with his teeth (sharp as razors, inhuman, animal teeth, all fangs, like a shark), I see the blood pouring out of me, and then I'm lying on my back in the sand, literally being split open by Orlando and others like him - three or four

At this point, he has become 4-legged, with the airbrushed-white face of a wolf-bird and the body of a dog. At the time I had no awareness of Anubis, but this was the form Orlando had taken. His helpers were of similar form, perhaps slightly smaller. I have never had more than a passing interest in Egyptology, so this manifestation seemed to come out of the blue.

As my body is opened from throat to pubis, he stands on all four legs in the center of me, devouring my mortal organs, tearing out the internal parts of me and tossing them to the others who stand nearby. I am literally consumed from the inside out, and as Orlando is ingesting what I perceive to be my heart, he lifts his head and looks me in the eyes, my blood running over his lips, my body inside his animal belly.

When our eyes meet, I sense that he is loving what he is doing - more than that, he loves devouring me, and that he is mildly surprised by this. I sense that the thought had occurred to him to leave me as dead, but because he loves the heart of me, down to a level of pure energy, I am deemed worthy of being allowed to live.

Images abound of the others also partaking in the feast of me, all wolf-bird creatures who dismember one self in order to recreate another. And yet, this is not Anubis destroying the heart of one found unworthy. Instead, it is an act of transformation, transmutation, transcendence. It is the power of the underworld acting directly on the mortal self - perhaps because the mortal Self intended it at some level of awareness, whether conscious or otherwise.

This is the shaman's destiny. The is the raising of oneself from the dead, the lifting of oneself out of the phantom's sleep and into the waking awareness of the infinite.

After I am totally devoured and only my skin remains - an empty husk devoid of organs and even bones and muscle - splayed on the sand and laid open as a deer hide would be laid open - the Orlando-beast (now the more familiar human-esque manifestation again), dives inside the still-warm skin and pulls it around him like a cape. Before I realize what's happening, he folds my skin around him, wrapping himself inside it, then begins rapidly sewing himself into it, using sinew and a wooden needle. Inside my skin, a new self rises onto the underworld beach and begins to dance to the sound of distant drumming.

At this point, I bounce back into some manner of ordinary awareness and write down notes on what happened. I conclude with the word *Skinwalker*? Though I'm strangely pleased at what's happened I'm also disturbed by the implications. On the one hand I realize I've been initiated into some larger world, some higher awareness, not unlike the passage that follows.

> *Once on the other side, the man will have to wander around. His good fortune would be to find a helper nearby - not too far from the entrance. The man has to ask him for help. In his own words he has to ask the helper to teach him and make him a diablero. When the helper agrees, he kills the man on the spot, and while he is dead, he teaches him.*
>
> *When you make the trip yourself, depending on hour luck, you may find a great diablero in the helper who will kill you and*

> *teach you.. After your return, you will not be the same man. You are committed to come back to see your helper often. And you are committed to wander farther and farther from the entrance, until finally one day you will go too far and will not be able to return...*
> —Carlos Castaneda, *The Teachings of Don Juan*

This dismemberment is described in many books, the ritual itself seeming to be a rite of passage when the initiate is taken apart in her human form and recreated using parts from the underworld itself. In most sources, the initiate sees herself being rebuilt with certain stones, crystals or healing plants. In my case, the shaman himself - the animal/man/Anubis - climbed inside my skin, so I am recreated as much "him" as "me".[10]

Beautiful, yet disturbing because it made me wonder if this was trying to tell me that I am Orlando's physicality. *Is it just me?* I wonder. *Has it been 'just me' all along?*

The riddle Orlando had whispered to me in the past repeated itself over and over. *You must be immortal before you will know how to become immortal.* By sewing himself inside my skin, was he giving me a part of his nature? Not physical immortality, but was this such a drastic shift of the assemblage point that I will now begin to see the world from an eternal perspective instead of such a narrow and limited first attention awareness alone?

Later, as I'm gazing out at the night, Orlando's voice comes to me across the expanse which seems to separate us, but an expanse which is only an illusion. *It's different for you now.*

---

[10] Editorial note: This event occurred before I had become aware that Orlando is my shamanic double. At the time, I was still functioning under the assumption that he was an entirely extant being. In fact, in the paragraphs that follow, you can see some of the developing thought-process that eventually led me to the Whole realization of exactly who and what Orlando is. This was not an easy revelation, nor a quick one.

That resonates, too, in a way that is both reassuring and terrifying for the sense of responsibility that accompanies it. There is no going back. There is no undoing what is done.

Nothing will ever be the same for I am no longer the same. The phantom self of the past lies in ashes on the shore of the underworld. The future is mine to create. The moment of creation may only be found in the Now.

At this time I still could not wholly conceive of the double, nor did I have adequate words to describe the experience. "The double" was only words in a book. I could not have conceived that the energy body is both male and female, and can take on any manifestation it might choose. Because it exists as an eternal being, it has access to All Knowledge, and can become our best teacher, if we are willing to start listening.

I am reminded of Castaneda's words:

> *I am now faced with the special problem of having to explain what it is that I am doing... and I must first of all reiterate that this is not a work of fiction. What I am describing is alien to us; therefore, it seems unreal.*
>
> -Carlos Castaneda, The Eagle's Gift

Without a doubt, this experience will sound like madness to those who have not experienced it.

Becoming a Diablero

> *"Once on the other side, the man will have to wander around. His good fortune would be to find a helper nearby - not too far from the entrance. The man has to ask him for help. In his own words he has to ask the helper to teach him and make him a diablero. When the helper agrees, he kills the man on the*

> *spot, and while he is dead he teaches him... but neither you nor they have the power to refuse..."*
> —Carlos Castaneda - *The Teachings of Don Juan*

October, 2009

This passage continues to find its way back into my awareness more often than could be considered coincidental, and though I have read this many times previously, it hit me with renewed strength when I came across it once again last night as I was working through some troublesome personal issues.

What don Juan didn't say to Carlos (perhaps because it was the old brujo's nature to reel his young apprentice in slowly rather than throwing out the whole hook, line and sinker) is that there also comes with that re-birthing process a responsibility and a Knowledge that can never be ignored from that moment forward.

I was indeed fortunate to meet a powerful brujo who killed me on the spot and made me a diablero[11]. More accurately, I would say that this incident opened the energetic pathways between the four compartments of my own double-beingness, and becoming a diablero (or sorcerer or brujo or shaman) is a process that is ongoing, and no one can "make" us anything. We can be handed the tools, which is what occurred that night, but the Doing is always up to each of us.

Whatever the technical explanation might be, the results are that I have found myself moving further and further away from this world - or, in don Juan's terms, further from the entrance, deeper into the otherworld, and at times there is less and less reason to return here. I have no regrets about this, though there is a certain sadness and melancholy at times.

It is the sadness of knowing those we love most may choose a phantom's path, the melancholy of realizing this is

---

[11] For those reading in random order, see the entry directly preceding this one entitled *"Initiation."*

truly a solitary journey, even when we walk it with other warriors or loving companions.

Over the course of time, I have encountered many sources who have made it known that this solitary path usually ends up costing the warrior everything we traditionally think of as normal: job, family, friends, lovers, and sometimes even our very life.

When Orlando first cautioned me about this, I must say I thought it would be different for me. Hah! Self-importance 101. But as time has gone by and I can now look back on a certain portion of the path, I must say that this is certainly turning out to be true. Those who were once my closest friends are now gone from my life - not because of a fundamental disagreement, but because as paths diverge it seems inevitable that the common ground is lost altogether. I cannot be content talking of recipes and child-rearing and passive entertainment, and the friends I once knew are too disturbed at the idea of walking through life with Death as one's advisor. And so it goes.

What comes to me as I'm writing this is the strong inclination to say to newbie warriors: be sure this is what you want. For myself, it is all I have ever wanted or desired, and on the night I was dismembered by my double and reassembled, I knew my world had changed forever. I would not go back even if I could, for now I am in love with the infinite, and my Intent is hooked to the nagual. And yet, I have watched others on this path who do end up regretting their choices, who end up wishing they didn't know any of this, wishing they could go back to their normal life. I have even watched some of them actively try to forget by absorbing themselves in every manner of distraction from drugs to real-life-role-playing. The danger is that once a warrior passes a certain point on the path, it simply isn't possible to undo what has been Done. If there is a limbo, a hell, surely that is it.

As I say, I simply feel compelled to put out the warning: *Be sure this is what you want, because you might not be able to find your way back again.* To me, the moment I became "lost" to the world was one of my greatest triumphs. But I will not say it is an easy path. There are those who would say nothing changes when a warrior wholly embraces the path, but that has not been my experience. There are those who would say we keep all our old friends and make new ones along the way, but that has not been my experience either. There are those who would say that as we become more spiritually aware and begin to engage our abilities, we will be loved by all those around us... but *that* has most definitely not been my experience.

I never forget that some of history's most enlightened brujos, shamans and people of Knowledge were shunned, persecuted, and even crucified or burned at the stake.

This path will not make anyone love you. It might make them turn on you. And it will definitely change your life and your relationships with those around you forever. Why? As we integrate ourselves and lose our own fragmentation, it is the natural instinct and mission of the world around us (the consensual reality) to make every attempt to bring us back in line with the status quo. If we don't realign with that status quo we are essentially identified as a threat and begin to be treated accordingly, rather like how the human immune system fights off invading viruses.

The problem is that this virus of Knowledge isn't a disease. It's the antidote. But "the body" doesn't recognize that. And so the warrior finds herself on a path that becomes paradoxically more solitary, and at the same time more vast and all-encompassing as it stretches toward the Infinite.

Choose the path wisely and only if it is from the heart. Have no regrets. And know you can never go home to Ixtlan again, for the food will have no taste, and the wine will have turned to vinegar, and the faces at the window will be phantom faces with hollow eyes and empty smiles.

Most of all, have no sadness in that. Instead, rejoice in all you Know.

The Birthday Gift

The wildflowers next to the lake were primarily yellow, rendered fluorescently more brilliant beneath a slate-grey sky which was threatening to drop rain. On the choppy surface of the water, a miniature pirate boat sailed through wisps of silver fog which manifested with the appearance of an army of ghosts dancing on the dusky blue surface.

Patrons of the Renaissance faire milled about in 15th century attire, while drums pounded a Middle Eastern rhythm not far away. A baby was crying; seagulls wailed mournfully; and my sandals rendered an odd squeaking sound as I made my way through the dew-slick grass. It occurred to me that it was my birthday. Made me chuckle to myself just a little - this arbitrary demarcation of time in an infinite sea of utterly meaningless moments. No difference whatsoever between yesterday, today and tomorrow, yet because we have been working these events for so long and I have become somewhat well-known among the other participants and merchants, I was greeted with smiles and the traditional calls of "Happy birthday!" as I made my way from one side of the faire to the other.

"Why are you so unhappy?"

I glanced up from where I had been looking at a patch of tree roots and dewdrops and spilled fairy dust, to find myself face to face with Kara - one of the psychics who does card and palm readings at the faire. At first, it didn't register that she had been speaking to me, but as our eyes met, she quickly brushed her own words aside, and added, "Not that it's any of my business, of course."

It surprised her that she had spoken, that much was immediately obvious, for her face flushed and she put a hand to her mouth as if to staunch her own words – not the typical mannerisms of a seasoned and self-assured crone.

What I found odd was how time slowed down and back-flipped and ran through its system of checks and balances. Presented with the question, I quickly ran an inventory, and came back with the realization that I was not unhappy in the least. Being a *seer* myself, it stands to reason that I can read Kara every bit as well as she believed she was reading me, and what I immediately saw in her was an edge of very real hostility tempered only slightly by genuine curiosity. Though we have been at most of the same events for the past several years, she is not someone with whom I have made a connection, and so to my perceptions, her question seemed to come straight out of that sky overhead.

What struck me was that she was *seeing* something about me, yet failing to understand *what* she was *seeing*, and so she could only interpret it in the traditional manner. She had read me as someone out of step with the usual drummers, and so her conclusion automatically became one of believing me to be unhappy. Not the first time this has happened - from family members to former friends. And, indeed, I suspect this is a pattern with most warriors who have been on their path for any length of time.

Because I had no reason to take her question personally, I stopped to talk with her. I told her first what she wanted to hear - for that's the stalker in me - which was the down and dirty truth that I was experiencing some physical pain from an old back injury, which is neither here nor there in the big picture. Just part of the inventory. That seemed to answer some question in her mind, for I saw her relax - and yet, even as we stood there with all the beauty of the lake surrounding us, I realized with a deep sense of Knowing that we were in two different realities.

Kara's definition of happy and mine are not the same - and so she could not reconcile within herself that my silence and preference to be alone do not automatically mean I am *un*happy. It occurred to me to attempt to explain my path to her, yet even as that thought crossed my mind, I knew it would be futile - for even though she is a psychic, she is not a seer, and there is a rather major difference. How could I tell her that the world is a vast, magnificent and mysterious stage peopled primarily by phantoms; and I am an immortal mortal who walks among them, knowing I am a being who is going to die.

To Kara, who talks a lot about love and light, my words would undoubtedly sound like the demented mumblings of a depressed schizophrenic. And yet, to my *seeing*, her love and light philosophy is only an extension of the illusions of the consensual reality – attempts to cheerfully enact a program many people choose to believe rather than any actual path based on experience and knowledge - and so again I found myself looking out over the lake and the wildflowers, having the very solid realization that her world and mine were literally worlds apart even though we were standing only inches away from one another, breathing the same crisp morning air.

The nagual has a habit of testing us, or perhaps it could be perceived that we put ourselves in the path of our tests. Had I walked down any other row that morning, I never would have encountered Kara; and there was something about the energetically-charged nature of her question that awakened me to the fact that this *was* a test. It wasn't Kara who was asking me why I was unhappy. It was mySelf asking the question by placing the words in the mouth of an extant being.

As I was standing there in that space between question and response, another long-time acquaintance passed by, smacked me unexpectedly on the rump, hugged me hard from behind, and planted a gruff kiss on my neck – far more intimate and familiar than I would have expected from this young man, but nonetheless sensual and erotically pleasant. "Happy birthday, ye ol' buccaneer," he said with a piratical grin – a reference to my attire. "If ye can't live forever, give 'em hell in heaven!"

Sounded like good advice. He embraced me a second time, ran his scruffy chin across my neck in a gesture that would have brought me to my knees 20 years ago, then disappeared with a hearty "Arrrgh!" into the morning mist with the long black feather from his 3-cornered hat bobbing along behind his tall, lean form.

I looked at Kara for a moment, her inquiry still ringing in my ears, and finally I simply said, "What's *inside* is good. It's the wrapper that's starting to fray a bit at the edges."

Her look said she didn't understand, and there wasn't enough time just then to explain the sorcerer's way, the shaman's path, the heartbeat of the eternal double in the body of the infinite. "Out of curiosity, what did you see that caused you to ask?" Another stalker trait – return the question to the questioner.

My inquiry seemed to surprise her, for her brows lifted, then furrowed. Her head tilted. "You walk alone, even when you're in a group," she said with a shrug, and seemed defensive for a moment. "I can't see your aura – or when I do, it's… black." She almost shuddered as she said the word.

And I knew then I had passed the test, for I felt a little smile tug at the corners of my lips and a raven swooped low, casting its shadow over my right shoulder. When I see a warrior, that is how they appear to me – like a cut-away in the fabric of reality, a shiny black egg that is reminiscent of a black hole: an anomaly so cohesive unto itself that not even light can escape.

That is the singularity of consciousness, Orlando's voice whispered in my ear, masquerading as a gust of wind blowing cold and unexpected off the surface of the lake. *The validation of it is my gift to you. Happy birthday, you ol' buccaneer.*

Not far away, silhouetted against the morning sun, the man who had embraced me only moments before stood looking in our direction, and for no reason whatsoever, bowed elegantly from the waist before turning to disappear into the crowd.

The nagual glinted on the dark surface of the lake, reflecting that which cannot be named, that which cannot be explained. In that glint is my joy and my sadness and all that *I-Am.*

That is my happiness.

Seeing and What is *Seen*

April 18, 2003

Seeing is directly connected to gnosis (silent knowing) in that it is what enables the warrior to always observe the truth of a situation even when that truth might appear on the surface to be obscured, or even as yet unrevealed.

How do I talk about *seeing*? I step outside my door, and the sapling greets me with fresh and fragile green leaves, and even if I had no calendar and no sense of time, I would *see* through the tree's eyes that it is spring and that it is time to grow, to sink my roots a little deeper into the earth and spread my branches a few inches further into the sky as I explore my world.

Somewhere deep in the dark, which is not the absence of light but the presence of night, a coyote and her pups are wailing joyfully into the cool air, and without knowing how I know, there is something in their song that reveals something about them. The pups are young and curious about this mysterious world, full of energy and hungry for life. And yet there is a sadness in Mother Yote's song, because she knows that soon it will be time to part from her pups, and though she has taught them well, she knows some of them will not live to see First Year. But she sings anyway, for those who will live and for those who will die, and her song is no different because each are equal in the end.

It isn't imagination that tells me these things, but Knowing... *Seeing*.. making a direct connection through the energetic structure (EM fields, if you prefer) with the same frequency that *is* the coyote's song or the young tree's springtime Intent. It is becoming one with what is traditionally considered as "other". It is experiencing the coyote's song in my own spirit that tells me what the words mean and why they are sung with such passion.

Overhead, a canopy of stars stretches out into the infinite, and each one has a story to tell about the things it has seen, the mysteries revealed by its light as that light probes without cessation or boundary, into the Infinite. To ride the starbeams is to experience eternity in an instant, for the light travels equally into past and future, generated always in the Now, seeking a surface upon which to reflect itself. A meteorite splits the darkness, like a knife cutting the sky in half, and to *see* that falling star is to *see* birth and creation simultaneously - the long journey through time which carried that piece of iron-nickel ore from some distant realm of space, where it was conceived in an implosion-explosion of matter countless eons in the past, to terminate here on Earth, matter returning to energy in flames, burning with the fire from within... and the feeling that this is exactly how it was Intended from the start and to the end, and there is no difference in that, either, for in returning to its component energy, the falling star continues the cycle whereby it will one day be part of a new blade of grass or a wildflower, or a coyote singing in the desert.

Sentience permeates all of it. And that is *seeing*, too. In the tree and the coyote and the falling star and the sand and the air, and all the emptiness of space that isn't empty at all, there is a powerful presence of Knowledge, the sentient universe thinking through all its billions of minds, which are all one mind in the end, yet comprised of billions of individuals, each as unique as a fingerprint, some conjoined to the Whole, others off on sabbaticals that may take millions of years, each one doing precisely what is within its desire and its will to be and to do. The sentience is the *seeing*, too, for it is through that sentience that we draw information and Knowledge about *what* we *see*.

Sometimes, out there in the void or deep in the heart of the warrior's inner silence, we encounter the unique, individual sentience which we recognize as the Self in eternity. And then we smile. Sometimes we even laugh out loud. And though we can't explain it, we know we've been talking to ourselves all along, looking at our own reflection in the stars and the tiny ponds on which their light is reflected throughout time and space.

There is no way to talk about *seeing*. So we talk about what we *see*.

Dragonfly

This afternoon as I was doing some work out on the carport, sorting through some things in preparation for our next business outing, I opened a large cloth sack which contains blankets and other items made of fabric. It was with some surprise that I found a small, perfectly preserved little dragonfly all rolled up inside a sheet. His wings were gossamer and green, and had curled under at the end, but still so shiny it was as if he had just stopped there to rest.

For a few moments, I just gazed at this dead creature with a sense of wonder, trying to recall where we might have picked him up, since his particular kind are not indigenous here in the desert. It took a bit before I recalled that our last outing had been to the Sacramento River area, and I did indeed recall seeing some dragonflies floating down the swift water poised on canoes made of fallen leaves or some bit of driftwood.

But even as I sat there in the late afternoon dusk, holding the mortal remains of this fragile creature in my hand, something happened that I cannot explain and will not even attempt to try. The dragonfly turned to a sprig of dried grass right there in my hand. Suddenly, it was not a dragonfly at all. Just a piece of brown, dead Bermuda grass that had obviously been rolled up in the sheet when we had packed down at the faire.

There is no doubt in my mind whatsoever that I was originally holding this dried-out but stunningly beautiful little insect. I examined the wings. I looked at the well-preserved compound eyes. I counted six little legs.

...and yet...

All that remained was a sprig of grass.

Embracing the Infinite

January 13, 2002

Late afternoon, 4:38 p.m. and long shadows lie gracefully on the ground, blending the end of day with the coming of night, a delicate tapestry of dusk. An unusual mist hangs in the air, recreating the distant mountains in shades of yellow and brown instead of the normal desert grays and purples of twilight.

Time seems frozen. Our Australian Shepherd sits outside my open door, facing the sunset with an almost Buddhist serenity. Distantly, unseen, a fruit bat calls into the crack between the worlds. On the road, a rickety pick-up rattles by, driven by an old Indian with long gray braids and a wide-brimmed hat, the elder shaman who has sometimes visited my visions.

The mist turns umber-orange at the level of the horizon, and the sun leaves the desert in the charge of gothic shadows and owl-song.

In a corner of my office, the tiny silver mouse who has made her home with us scratches at a piece of paper, a gentle rustling of life. I fear she will one day breed, yet despite the dictates of logic, I take no action against her. And so she honors our silent agreement by remaining childless, and we continue to peacefully co-exist.

Though there is no wind to speak of, the large pipe chime sounds a note or two, a temple bell instantly transforming my dark velvet room into a monastery and myself into a monk contemplating the gathering twilight on the tip of a pen.

The postcard perfect world outside this door knows no worries in this frozen Now. The Joshua trees are still, meditating on the passing of time, and even the telephone poles with their sagging wires seem at rest, silent sentinels mesmerized by the brisk chatter that erupts from a hummingbird to disrupt the stillness for a moment.

I find myself thinking of Orlando, remembering when we knew him all those years ago, before he disappeared and became an ally writing letters from the edge of the abyss. Sometimes over the years, I've tried to tell myself it was all just a big coincidence. It wasn't *really* sorcery, magic, manifestation of a lifetime of intent. "He was just a man," I've heard my own voice whisper, close to my ear. For it would make things so much easier if I could believe that.

And yet, at a level of Knowing that cannot be denied, I

fully realize that these are only the fearful retractions of someone who has seen a truth so vast it is overwhelming, even terrifying, in its intensity. We lie to ourselves because that truth is so often incomprehensible. Easier to pretend it never happened.

But it did.

And so the tumblers of comprehension always click and align, refusing to be ignored or cast into foreign shapes just so I might be able to sleep better at night, just so I could go back to being normal, just another phantom. There's no going back. Wouldn't even if I could. The truth is still the truth, transformative, and so Ixtlan[12] is always in the distance.

And he is still standing there in his white wicker living room, backlit by a streetlight shining through a rain-slicked window, asking the question that ended one world and will be forever creating a new one in its wake. *"Who are you?"*

If he were standing here now, perhaps I could finally answer. *I am the mountains and the mist that embraces them; the feather on the owl's wing and the coyote hymn echoing off the foothills as night finally falls. I am somewhere in the distance, nowhere in particular. I am myself and I am you and there is no difference.*

The ink dries on the page.

The world becomes a black silhouette.

A stray cat pauses in the long dirt driveway, and I am endlessly looking into the eyes of the ally.

---

[12] *Journey to Ixtlan*, by Carlos Castaneda. What is Ixtlan? In this book, it is represented as an *idea* of a place that exists only in our minds, even though it is a real place in Mexico. When we think of going "home," the reality is never the same as how we remember it. The problem the warrior-seeker faces is that there are always "phantoms on the road to Ixtlan" - those well-meaning souls who want us to join them in their illusory beliefs.

Facing the Hummingbird[13]

January 7, 2003

I spent the morning holding an 18 year old cat in my arms while he struggled to live, struggled to die, and ended up somewhere in between. At first I fidgeted. Hours passed. I had taken him out in the sun, for even though I am not a sun-worshipper, this wasn't about what *I* wanted or didn't want, what I could or couldn't do with my own abilities. It wasn't about my own will, but about the will and intent of another life form, a different species whom we tend to think of as being so different from ourselves as to often seem alien altogether, and yet I am convinced that consciousness is simply consciousness. How it manifests and expresses itself in matter is really the only difference.

As I sat there holding this sadly decrepit animal in my arms, there were moments when it occurred to me to simply pack him in the car and take him to the vet, where a quick injection would send him on his eternal journey. And yet, at a level of communication that transcends species, I knew this was not what *he* wanted. In some way that I cannot communicate, he asked me to let him face the eagle in his own good time, and because he has always been a warrior, I could not deny him that request.

And so we sat there together on the porch. I talked to him about the day. Sky so blue it was almost painful to gaze upon, a few puffy white clouds, drifting over at a visible rate of speed. A cactus wren was complaining that the bird feeder was empty, but when she looked over and saw us, she fell into a reverent silence.

Shadows had pooled beneath the piñon pines and Joshua trees, and for a moment they turned 3D - actual energy-reflections of their physical counterpart. There was no

---

[13] "Facing the Hummingbird" originally appeared in Quantum Shaman: Diary of a Nagual Woman.

difference between the raven and his shadow, and so I told Myrrh that it would soon be time for him to inhabit his shadow. In the air all around me, I was watching specks of light dancing like a gathering of fireflies. At first, I thought they were just a trick of the light, some anomaly of physical vision. The things we tell ourselves in our internal dialog to keep the world properly assembled

    I found myself in a dilemma as I talked to my cat-companion of 18 years about where he was going and what he might see. Do I really Know with certainty that what I am saying is true? Is there really a continuity of consciousness beyond this life, based on cohesion of identity, or is that, like angels and devils, just another belief system? Even though I have had experiences with a world beyond the veil of this mortal illusion, I was forced to concede that all those experiences came while still attached to this mortal body. Is the body the projector of consciousness, or only a temporary receptacle? Arguments could be found for either point of view, and at that moment while this fragile creature was dying in my arms, I could have argued either side with equal and vehement conviction.

    For awhile, I simply drifted on this wave of contemplation until I entered into a deep trance state. The energy beams had mesmerized me, carried me away on their electric wings. And so I flew with them for a time, trying to make sense of it all. The turmoil I had been feeling slowly dissipated. The internal dialog which had been yammering previously realized it was being observed, and fell into silence.

    A hummingbird fluttered close to my face. Spirit-carriers they're called in some cultures - guardians whose task it is to lead or carry the spirits of the dead to the source of creation in the otherworld, where the eternal river of consciousness has its source. I smiled to myself, finding it appropriate to think of Myrrh chasing a hummingbird guardian into Eternity.

    Time passed. Yet there was no time at all. The Now extended infinitely in all directions. A single moment became

All moments. And somewhere in all of the chaos of the world, somewhere in all of the turmoil of my own thoughts, it all just stopped and I realized that I had joined with my own eternal other. Those words are completely inadequate, a pathetic attempt to describe what must simply be experienced. I found myself Whole, inhabiting the assemblage point that is infinitely familiar to me, yet which I have actually experienced only a few times in my life. I could say I joined with Orlando, but that would make it sound as if two came together into one. And while that was part of it, it was not *all* of it. Ultimately, all I can say is that I found the assemblage point of Eternal Whole Self for those few moments. Like a peek behind the curtain, a gnostic certainty that when we embrace that assemblage point, all is indeed eternally well.

Somewhere or somewhen, Time started forward again. Maybe a horn honked. Maybe a coyote sang. Back in ordinary awareness, I was left with a sense of once again Knowing there is more to the human (or animal) spirit than we have ever been allowed to believe from within the consensual agreement. Even if consciousness is initially only a projection of the physical body, then I can only conclude that consciousness *becomes* the projector for the Spirit, and the Spirit becomes eternally cohesive (inhabiting the *I-Am* of an eternal identity) through the process of conjoining itself to the indestructible energy body in the same way consciousness initially conjoined itself to these organic bodies.

Just rambling, trying to wrap comprehension around the infinite. Silly attempt. But nonetheless an attempt that must be made from the heart while the hummingbirds are sitting quietly in the locust trees, and the old grey warrior sleeps in my lap, slowly entering his own eternal dream, inhabiting his own immortal shadow.

May the sun make your shadow strong and the moon free your spirit to Dream.

Snow Play

January 29, 2002

Outside my door, a light snow is falling, random flakes drifting and playing in unseen currents. Unconsciously, my eyes go out of focus and I am staring at a spot of emptiness perhaps five feet in front of me. In the distance, cold grey clouds hug bleak, desolate mountains, snowy squatters obscuring the peaks. Closer, inside my own yard, ocotillos tremble in the rare and precious chill.

In that empty space where I am focused, I watch energy dancing – particles of light swirling like hundreds of ice skaters playing on a frozen pond, each going in a different direction, circling drunkenly, faster and faster, yet never seeming to collide, as if the perfect choreographer has orchestrated the frenzied flow.

I am aware of a single snowflake, larger than the rest, plummeting to the ground as if it simply folded its white wings and dropped, eager for its journey to be over. My mind notes this, but thinks nothing of it. Then, in the silence of this unintentional meditation, the voice of silent knowing whispers in my ear, *Look! It will happen again!* And though I have no expectations, still focused on the dancing, circling particles of light, the same suicidal snowflake plummets through the same space in the icy air to impact in the same spot of desert sand where its own pale ghost still lies melting.

My mind quickly tries to explain it away – water dripping from overhead wires, or a mere random coincidence.

The voice of gnosis only chuckles. *We could show you again, but would you believe it even then?*

And so it showed me again. The same snowflake, the same trajectory, the same plop. I know what I saw. The question is: what does it mean? Why does the same leaf fall three times for Carlos Castaneda? Why does the same snowflake obliterate itself more than once? Is it only so we can *see* it? And having *seen* it, what is the lesson?

On the western horizon, there is a break in the clouds and sun filters through the mist, dappling the mountains. I ache for the storm to remain, revealing its secrets not easily seen in the brighter haze of a common sunny day.

Tiny droplets of water pool and bead on the cushion of a lawn chair, and a cactus wren comes to drink the shiny diamonds, suckling nourishment from the melted snow. The fire in my fireplace crackles, pine smoke curling over the roof to sneak back in through the open door so it may draught up through the chimney again and over the roof and back through the door, an endless cycle fueled by the intent of the fire. Grey ghosts hurry down the driveway, startling shy quail.

In an act of sorcery that has come to be its own exegesis, I scatter the ashes of last night's fire along the path from my door to the road. I hear a voice and recognize it as my own – the voice of the witch, the shaman's breath. "From the ashes of this mortal self, I call upon the Whole *I-Am* already a part of eternity. Come to me. Teach me so that I may become what you are – the whole potential of the evolved Self."

Just words. Meaning nothing to anyone but me. Fodder for those who would say I'm just a crazy old woman tossing her own ashes into the wind, talking to herself in a snowstorm. Ah, yes. Talking to herself. The shaman's double who is already evolved and outside of time. I do talk to him, luring him to come and teach me how to become what he himself already is – so that I may evolve sufficiently to place him outside of quantum time so that he may teach me... like the pine smoke caught in its own energy, creator and created conjoined, each seeking its own source which can always be found in the other – the self made Whole.

A voice at the edge of the road asks, *What do you bring to the infinite aside from this trail of ash?*

The wind is brisk, cold, sentient. Tires caress the wet street, just carriages driven by phantoms who do not seem to even perceive me.

"I bring the fire and the smoke, and the Knowledge that each is only a manifestation of the other," I reply.

A shudder passes through me, and I feel Orlando smile – a dangerous, alluring grin comprised of thrice-fallen leaves and ice crystals gathering on the bow of an old sailing ship where we have met and joined before.

After a pause in the storm, the snow resumes, sneaking in at the crack between the worlds.

———

The Fall To Earth

November 8, 1999

I dream of being thrown down to Earth – coming from somewhere else into this mortal life, seemingly as some sort of punishment or imprisonment. In the dream, to become human is to drink of Lethe, to forget what we are and therefore to become trapped in human rules – mortality, death, decay, loss of eternal consciousness. In this dream, I am fighting to remember, trying to hold on to some sense of my immortal identity, fighting to hold memory intact because there was someone I loved very dearly in that other life, someone who was also being thrown to Earth.

As I fall into this earthly realm, I see it from above – a writhing mass of humans on a sandy white beach. I feel my previous identity dissipating. I will not be able to fight to remember because I will forget there was ever anything *to* remember. The closer I get to the beach, the more I feel myself dissipating, becoming just another amnesiac prisoner on the shore which seems so beautiful, but which is really the entry point into this terrible prison.

As I am about to touch the ground, I fight horribly to hold onto the face of my lover, whom I know has also been cast down to Earth, for I tell myself that if I can find him/her again, together we can remember who and what we were before, and somehow we can destroy the illusory prison in order to return ourselves to eternity as immortal companions.

It is morning on Earth, the crowded shore so beautiful and alive with so many faces of so many people, yet I am filled with horror and dread. I look around, realizing I once knew all of them, yet now they are only strangers, forgetful prisoners, given a life sentence from which there is no parole, no appeal, only escape if at all possible, yet the greater horror is the realization that a prisoner will attempt no escape unless he realizes he *is* a prisoner. If he cannot see the bars, if the prison looks like Hawaii or Greece or Joshua Tree, and the entertainment is designed to last a lifetime and be experienced as Reality, one very quickly loses any idea that he is in prison at all. Trapped in a solitary confinement cell of flesh – the mortal body – the prisoner is made to feel that the larger prison (the exterior world) and even his individual cell are natural, and so he acquiesces without struggle into prison life – which is really nothing more than a lifetime of dying.

But as I ask myself why this would be done, why would we be imprisoned in such a manner, why would we be cast out of the immortal kingdom and not just killed outright, the answer is clear and succinct: *An immortal soul cannot be killed, but it can die if it can be made to believe it is mortal.*

So rather than trying to kill what cannot be killed, we are placed in mortal bodies in a prison of pretty illusions, where we slowly die because we *believe* we will. The nature of the prison is to slowly destroy the immortal soul - and in general it seems to take about 70-90 years for it to die a natural human death.

Upon waking , I did not at first remember this dream, and only when I caught one image of the beach at dawn was I able to recall it at all. Truly a shamanic dream, perhaps even a major breakthrough, for the dream not only reminds me that we are in a prison of both physical mortal flesh and illusory bars we think of as external reality, it also points out that we are more than these mortal bodies, and we did have consciousness and eternal life before we were banished here for reasons I cannot begin to imagine. An insane ruler among the immortals who cast out anyone who might have been perceived as a threat? An upheaval of the immortal kingdom by forces or invaders coming in from outside? A war in heaven? Is this why such myths abound in human literature? Is there a vague spark of our memory that can't be destroyed? Is this why we feel our very soul dying as we fall deeper and deeper into the mandatory illusion of this life – job, responsibility, obligations to others even above obligations to the self?

To call it a vast, evil conspiracy is to break one of the prison's primary rules - and so to even suggest it is to be labeled insane and ignored. The prison is flawless for the wardens are ourselves. The only way out is to escape ourselves, to become more than our human thinking by being *outside* of that thinking. Is this why the forbidden fruit is forbidden? Is this why shamans are persecuted and destroyed – because they *do* occasionally see beyond the prison and threaten to destroy the whole damn thing by staging a revolt and leading a massive escape?

It is sad to see the prison and to know we are all dying because mortal life is nothing more than a slow-functioning gas chamber for the destruction of the immortal soul. I do not feel I am a dog trying to become a fish. Instead, I am a fish who has been made to believe he is a dog so he will naturally life his life out of water and slowly die as a result! I am a fish trying to shed the false nature of the dog so that I can simply return to what I have always been before I was banished from the sea and falsely imprisoned in a dog suit! I am an eternal being struggling to cast off this lethal illusion of mortality before the immortal soul slowly asphyxiates as a result of truly believing it is a mortal mechanism.

We are thrown down from heaven with the trash and left to die a "natural" death, for clearly the only way to destroy a true immortal is to convince him he is mortal. I am starting to remember – for in this dream I remembered the fall to Earth and I remembered, quite simply that there was something *to* remember. I was *I-Am* before I became a prisoner of this mortal illusion. And if the only way to regain my immortality is to destroy the illusion itself by smashing the projector, so it shall be.

A Glimpse of the Allies

May 26, 2003

Last night, as Wendy and I were coming home extremely late from a much-needed night of R and R, I was drifting in and out of a light sleep-state in the passenger seat. The night was extremely dark, and either the moon had already set, or was obscured behind a light cloud cover, so when we turned onto a side street that eventually leads toward the house, the only light was that of our headlights bouncing along the deserted road. As I was coming out of my alpha-state, I opened my eyes and took a quick glance around to determine our location.

What caught my eye was movement on the side of the road - two men pushing a bicycle and some other form of cart, possibly a shopping cart, along the curb on the opposite side of the street. Because they were approximately 100 feet away when our headlights first caught them, they appeared as dark silhouettes cut into the darker fabric of the night - black on black. My immediate thought was that they were probably folks who live in one of the nearby apartment buildings, walking home after a late night of carousing at the Memorial Day carnival which drifted into town on a dark wind.

But as the car moved closer, and my assemblage point moved from the gnostic-trance state and back into ordinary reality, the headlights revealed only a deserted street. The shadows were gone, as if they had never been there at all. I watched this happen quite calmly and with complete awareness, as my mind moved through the various assemblage points. When first opening my eyes, I was still in the gnostic state, and was therefore relying on what amounts to a different set of preceptors. I was assembling other worlds, where a couple of allies were out for a late-night stroll, probably for no other reason than to see if anyone might notice. But as I settled back in the world of ordinary awareness and once again assembled this world quite by habit, I literally saw the shadows vanish.

In reality, of course, the allies were still there. It was only my perception that had changed. But what I found amazing was that we usually don't have the luxury of perceiving such an event from start to finish, with full awareness. Normally, we tend to witness an event, then attempt to explain it through hindsight, and we usually end up settling for the logical explanation that we were either dreaming or (my personal favorite) "it was a trick of the light." Light is such a tricky bastard. Stays up late figuring out ways to trick us.

There is no explanation for what I saw last night. That's the power of the nagual.

Catching Sharks with Tweezers

April 12, 2008

Trying to comprehend the machinations of the unknown is rather like trying to catch a shark with tweezers. So, with what said, the event I am going to describe here is simply a description of something that occurred yesterday - recorded only in the interests of providing a record so that patterns can be examined over a period of time.

~

It was hot. Too hot. Wendy was sick with a cold and I had gone out into an unfamiliar town to do some errands in preparation for our event this weekend. Found a large outdoor shopping center which had all the things I might need: Trader Joe's, major grocery store, Chinese food for lunch, and a drug store - plus all of the accompanying smaller gift shops and the like.

So I parked at one end of the large complex and began my errands. In the Trader Joe's, it occurred to me that people were unusually friendly - several strangers not only spoke to me in a casual manner, but three of them actually started up full blown conversations. I didn't think too much of it, just finished up my shopping and moved on to the Chinese restaurant to order take-out for Wendy, who had stayed in the motor home back at the event site.

Upon finishing up that chore, I began walking toward the far end of the parking lot - the equivalent of about 2 city blocks - when I looked up to see one of the shops that jutted out and formed a corner was a tuxedo shop. *Friar Tux.* Cute name, I thought.

But then anything normal was plucked away like so much window dressing, and I found myself straddling some peculiar fence between one world and another. No other way to describe it. I was my normal "Della-self" standing there on the sidewalk looking at the tux shop in the middle of a hot, sunny afternoon. And at the same time, I had become a *different* Della-self standing on the same sidewalk, staring at the same tux shop, except to *that* self's perception, it was now dusk, and Orlando had just walked out of the shop, dressed in some incredible tux and looking like a perfect groom plucked from the pages of GQ.

So my normal Della-self is observing this while the parallel Della-self is experiencing it as if it is every bit as real as anything else. Orlando meets my eyes and smiles warmly - a smile of familiarity, affection, gladness. Walking over to me, he places one hand on my arm - the touch is warm, firm, solid. Not a ghostly vision. Not an old woman's fond remembrances. Real. Solid. Whole.

Leaning down close to my ear - so close I could smell the scent of a fine cologne and feel his breath on my neck - he whispered, "I'm still 28."

When I knew Orlando in the flesh, he was 28, so the reference made sense.

And then, as quickly as I had been displaced in the time/space continuum like so much energetic fluff, I was back in my ordinary awareness, standing there on that too-hot sidewalk, wondering what the hell just happened.

My heart was racing. I could barely breathe. And yet, nothing at all seemed out of the ordinary. It wasn't a stroke. It wasn't a heart attack. It was just the nagual having a party on the outskirts of parallel perception.

Upon returning to the motor home I began to realize that there had been indicators *prior* to the actual displacement.

Back in Trader Joe's, the first stranger who spoke to me was an old man, who addressed me in the manner of someone who already knows me. "How have you been?" he asked, and began talking in such a way that I had thought it odd at the time, but hadn't yet put the pieces together. It wasn't *as if* the old man knew me. He *did* know me. We spoke only briefly, but it was clear this wasn't just some nice old man and a case of mistaken identity. That's what I had believed at the time, but in light of other things, it now seems unlikely.

The second stronger who approached me at Trader Joe's did so at the bread aisle. Walking up to me as if he knew me, he boldly said, "Isn't it terrible how all the breads in the regular stores are laced with so much sugar?" He might as well have been reading my mind, for that's what I'd been thinking as I stood there reading the labels. He went on to make a comment to the effect, "We're conditioned to crave sugar because it's in everything we eat, but for those of us who are diabetic, it's a huge issue!"

At the time, I thought perhaps he was referring to himself as a diabetic. After all, he was a stranger, and there was no way he could know anything about me or my medical history. So I conversed with him in a friendly manner, and figured perhaps the people of this town had just become unduly friendly over the six months since I had last been here.

At the checkout counter, the elderly gay clerk was so friendly and outgoing, one might have thought I was his long lost sister. "You folks are going to be out at the park this weekend, aren't you?" he asked. Now, my tonal brain being fully engaged, I figured he was someone who had been to the Renaissance faire in the past and just recognized me. So I struck up a conversation with him about the weather and the preparations which were underway, but throughout the dialog, I kept thinking that he was extremely familiar.

In hindsight I can either write it off as the lunatic ravings of a madwoman, or I can look at these events from the eyes of a warrior, and see that perhaps one of those doorways I've been looking for opened a crack, and allowed me to catch a glimpse of some parallel self, some alter-world where I am me but not me, where I must live here in this city instead of in the desert - actually not far from where I *did* live when I knew Orlando in manifestation.

I'm still 28.

I've been thinking about that message and what it might mean. What it really seems to be saying to me is that the double is ageless and timeless, and that nothing has changed since he and I were last here in this place where we never were at all when we were walking around together back in the late 80s and early 90s. Inside the hologram which exists outside of time he *is* still 28, and I am the consort to the muse which can never be caught, and everything is unfolding precisely as it should, even if I cannot wrap my ordinary-humanform mind around some of these strange twists and turns on the road which exists only after we walk it.

There is no conclusion, for none is possible.

There is only the experience itself, and Rod Serling somewhere in the shadows of that forever-dusk world, reminding us that the world is not only stranger than we imagine, it is often the door to *The Twilight Zone*, even in broad daylight on a hot afternoon in Escondido.

Conundrum

September 5, 2002

Last night in a shamanic journey, I found myself in a quandary of conflicts which came as a bit of a surprise. The spirit wanted the journey, but the body was refusing to relinquish its assemblage point of security (a completely false illusion), and as a result, the experience quickly deteriorated to a point where no forward motion was possible, and going back the way I had come was equally restricted because of the presence of the ally, plus to do so would have violated my own intent. By my own designs, I had trapped myself, and though it was mightily unpleasant at the time, perhaps that was as it needed to be in the long run.

For a long time, I floundered, as the voice of the logos said, *Show me your cohesion.* Searching for it, I could not find it. All of existence and consciousness appeared to be little more than fragments of unconnected events, memories like separate bubbles, having little significance without the linear connecting line that passes for personal identity in first attention. I was a speck of chaos in an unforgiving and unforgivable void. Even the connection to Orlando seemed to be nonexistent as I wrestled with the idea of calling 911 and begging them to take me to some well-lit hospital where I might be given the antidote to this dreadful awareness, to this terrible sense of feeling lost even in the midst of knowing beyond doubt who and what *I-Am*.

Of course, the price of the shaman's journey is to know that there is no antidote, and that even if one were to find one, it would only shove one back into the peaceful contentment of the program. The journey is real, but Ixtlan as it is normally perceived in first attention is only an illusion, and all the travelers along the way phantoms. At the time while I wrestled with this conflict between body and spirit, it seemed I would certainly die. Not at some nebulous point in the future. Not tomorrow. But *Now*. It would all simply stop, and the universe would have a grand cackle at the frailty of the human condition, the eagle would lick his talons clean, and that would be the end of it.

Attempting to describe the descent into the nagual would be pointless, except to say that it left me with a keen awareness that something was *wrong*. My body wanted to interpret this as physical danger to itself. The spirit could only interpret it as an inability to assemble cohesion. There was no single assemblage point of *I-Am*, but instead a roller coastering through a plethora of worlds, a million divergent points of awareness which held no special significance. Remembering this. Thinking that. Observing the creation and destruction of the universe, but only as a matter of fact rather than with the formation of any individual opinion. It was the incarnation of chaos, yet even Chaos would have held more cohesion that what I was observing.

I reached out for Orlando, but there was just the void echoing back from the abyss, mocking me for ever daring to think I had achieved Wholeness. On one level of awareness, I knew, of course, that he was there. And yet, I could not reach him, could not enter that assemblage point of the Whole Self even though there was undeniable awareness of its existence. My body was in distress – tightness in the chest, increased heart rate – all of which were only attempts at distraction, dissipation. The consensual reality expressed in simple organic terms. Feed me. Take care of me. Reassure me. Petty demands of the tyrant.

Struggling for impeccability, I finally sank into the silence between each individual incarnation of chaos, drifting between the bubbles. From there, it was easily known to me that my body was not really in distress. Like a child throwing a tantrum, it was merely vying for attention. Slowly, from within that silence, the cohesion found me, yet only when I stopped looking for it, only when I stopped trying to define it.

Then and only then, Orlando was there. Then and only then, I joined with my Whole Self. Then and only then, I realized he had been laughing at me all along, watching me flounder, and with unconditional love, doing nothing to interfere. It occurred to me to slap him, but since that would have involved slapping myself at that moment, the idea quickly lost its luster.

For a long time, we simply enjoyed the contact, the Wholeness, the identity that rises above the chaos only when it is finally perceived that the chaos is the myriad worlds of the myriad fragments of the self, each one struggling for its own sovereignty, each one doomed to the eagle unless and until that Wholeness can be realized and inhabited through will and intent.

Finally, exhausted, I fell asleep, and awoke this morning to find myself back in this familiar world. Going about my usual morning routines for awhile, I pondered the events of last night, feeling restless and unsettled despite the eventual positive outcome. The logos was whispering in my ear again. Now, it said very clearly, *You have to find your way home to Ixtlan*. Knowing that Ixtlan is entirely fictional even if it exists as a real physical place, just as don Genaro knew it, the inference was that I needed to find my way home to the source of this journey – the things that fuel my heart and make my spirit sing.

Recently, so much of the journey has turned to an intellectualization of what is a truly mystical, magical and inexplicable trek into the unknown. Trying to wrap words around it can only limit it.

Sitting down in front of my altar (my indulgence for ritual) I lit the red candles and settled myself into a meditation which quickly revealed to me the pure definition of "energy efficiency". This comfortable silence felt good. It felt right. Outside my door, thunder tumbled across the desert and rain chattered on the roof, a brief respite from a long and dangerous drought. Real magic crept in through the open window, down the dormant chimney. A raven told tales of power from high atop a nearby telephone pole. The power was real, and it was all around me. And because of that, the energy it produced was far beyond anything that can ever be generated through intellectual pursuits alone.

You can't try to be him, you just have to let him be, the logos said, referring to the connection between myself and Orlando. That is the cohesion. That is the state of Wholeness. It cannot be sought or chased after. It cannot be tied up neatly with words and made to fit in a box of explanations someone else might be able to grasp. It can only be experienced, and then only when one is at peace, neither pursuing nor retreating, simply stalking oneself with long-term intent. And maybe, if one is extremely fortunate, some small portion of it can be understood and scribbled about in this dark-bound journal.

It is one thing to understand the nature of shamanic magic. It is another thing to be able to communicate that to others. But it is another world entirely to actually engage with the magic, to gather the fiery filaments of will and intent at the apex of heart and solar plexus, and simply feel the mystical state of mind. Only then are we free, but it is a freedom that must be fought for and maintained on a daily basis, and it is a freedom that does not thrive on intellect alone.

We have to get our hands dirty with the actual Doing, or else the journey is just analysis, intellectual masturbation, misdirected drivel. I ask myself what brought me on this path in the first place, and instantly my mind flashes back to an 11 year old girl shaking her fist at the sky and avowing to the heavens, "If I can't come to you, I'll bring you to me!" An oath to the nagual which still echoes out there somewhere, an echo that constantly rewards as long as I remember to keep shouting into the void.

The Ally

This morning I had to make a journey into the city to return a rental car Wendy and I had used on our recent road trip. She was in the rental, and I was following behind in our Suburban. During the course of traveling, a car got between us, and then began to drive slower... and slower... and slower. Finally I had had enough, and after a thorough check of the road and my surroundings, gunned the engine and pulled around the old Camaro in an attempt to pass.

It stands to reason that he immediately sped up, and a driveway which would have been no danger had he *not* sped up suddenly loomed ahead as a pick-up pulled up to the road with the obvious intention of turning right, which would have put him in a head-on situation with me. Indeed, it is doubtful he even looked in my direction, since the oncoming traffic would have been from the opposite direction.

Time began to slow down, and the thought went through my head that this was it. No way out. Nowhere to go. After all, the guy in the driveway was already pulling onto the two-lane desert highway, the car I was passing wasn't about to slow down *or* speed up, and so I found myself driving down the road with Death sitting in the passenger's seat, one eyebrow raised, asking, *Well, what are you going to do, bruja?*

For someone who knew she was about to die in a most gruesome manner, I was surprisingly calm, and Time had ceased to exist. I recall taking a breath, the feel of my hands on the steering wheel, the haze hanging over Mt. San Jacinto... and I knew there was very little I *could* do. I was continuing to speed up, hoping to skate past the Camaro, though I was also keenly aware that if the gamble failed, it would also mean a much higher-speed impact, head-on.

It's impossible to describe how sharp and clear perception becomes in this kind of situation. I was thoroughly aware of my surroundings, right down to the housefly buzzing against the windshield, as if he, too, sensed his end coming. Just the pick-up in the driveway, myself, and the speeding idiot I had been attempting to pass. And a lone raven sitting on a telephone pole like some detached witness.

But suddenly, as if appearing out of nowhere, there was a man walking down the side of the road. Never saw his face. All I know is that he walked directly in front of the pick-up, forcing the driver to stop to allow him to pass. There is no sidewalk on this deserted stretch of road. And there was nowhere the man could have come from nearby. Just a stranger walking down the road in the middle of nowhere on an inconsequential Wednesday morning. A man who had definitely *not* been there a moment before.

It was only because of the appearance of that stranger that I'm writing this right now. Because the man caused that truck to stop for no more than 5 seconds, I had the time to slip in front of the Camaro, while my Death sat there grinning, shrugging one bony shoulder, and sighing softly as he went back to gazing out the window where fields of windmills were spinning shadows on shifting desert sands. *Did you just get lucky, or did you summon that ally?* he asked matter-of-factly.

Damned if I know.

When I looked in the rearview mirror, the pick-up was pulling onto the highway, and the ally was nowhere to be seen.

The wind blowing in off the nagual is cold tonight, and the sky is crisp and full of stars.

―――

John Edwards and Mediumship

Over this past weekend, Wendy and I went to a seminar given by John Edward, the medium who does the syndicated show, *Crossing Over*. I had watched his show on and off over the past couple of years, and though I was skeptical, I have come to believe he is as close to authentic as one is likely to find.

What surprises me is that this surprises me. Because of my own numerous experiences with what most folks with consider "the mystical" (but to me is my everyday life), I found myself sitting in the audience feeling displaced and almost out of body - much the same as a feeling I have come to associate with the assemblage point of shamanic vision quests. Indeed, it was as if the energy in the room - a blend of anticipation and hope and grief and love - was transformative and palpable all on its own.

The seminar itself was largely what I had expected- a sell-out crowd at the Hollywood Palladium. The interesting thing about watching John work was that I also came to see that he is using the same form of gnosis which I use in my own life. In Toltec terms, it is the place of silent knowing closely associated with *seeing*. There was a recent discussion at one of my get-togethers that could have been titled *Is the Universe Made of Information?* My own experience is that it most definitely is. Any answer to any question can be found within that sentient web, for the information itself comes from the combined knowledge and experience of everything that has ever lived or ever will - not just on this planet, but throughout the universe, into the eternal and the infinite. The ancient Gnostics were clearly tapping into this universal awareness, just as the Toltecs have done, and undoubtedly the greatest mystics of all systems of Knowledge.

As I was observing John Edward, largely through the eyes of heightened awareness (I had intentionally slipped into an altered state, just one step above trance-awareness), I began to see and hear some of the things he was seeing and hearing. As he was reading a woman in the balcony who had lost her daughter, I immediately saw a glimpse of a plane crash and a high school girl in a cheerleading outfit. And, as it turns out, the woman's daughter had indeed died in a plane crash on the way to a cheerleading competition. Though it was never revealed one way or the other, my impressions were of the plane that went down off the coast of New York several years back.

Sometimes, I think this path has become so commonplace to me that I can forget how truly wondrous it really is. So in that way alone, I got far more than the price of admission.

What was brought to mind, however, was the old question of *what* it is that mediums read. Some postulate that they are reading the living - but in my own experience, and watching John work, I don't think so, because all too often, something will come out that the person being read knows nothing about, and is only able to validate at some later time. Which leads me back to the concept of gnosis, and the universe as information, the holographic universe, in which all experience, knowledge, awareness is stored as holographic bits of data which someone who has learned to *see* can glean with just a reasonable amount of dedication and practice.

So what - exactly - is the medium *seeing*? Is it the living essence of someone who has crossed over, or is it the holographic imprint of the life they lived - like a home movie playing eternally on the fabric of the infinite?

Personally, I have no doubt that consciousness can and does survive as cohesive units of *I-Am* awareness beyond this life - particularly when a certain level of awareness and ability has been achieved during life. And, indeed, even John Edward has said that he cannot make contact with everyone who has ever crossed over. Only certain energies seem strong enough to be read, though at times those stronger energies seem to pull others through with them - rather like a computer linking to a network to make additional information available.

The experience left me with a great sense of awe and renewed wonder, so it seemed appropriate to approach the questions from a warrior's perspective. Do mediums actually read the living-eternal-consciousness of those who have crossed over, or are they reading an autobiography stored in the holographic universe? Something to think about.

———

Double Vision[14]

October 12, 2004

It was a weekend of sensory overload, a noisy generator on one side, and the clatter and clamor of drums and belly dancers on the other, offset by a crowd of 100,000 Renaissance patrons and participants, all of whom seemed to be in a tremendous hurry to be somewhere other than where they were, even though they had paid a fair amount of money to be *precisely* where they were. My cold had turned to the flu. The assemblage point shifts in delirium. A cacophony of unrelated colors and shapes. A din of heat. An ice-cream flavored swirl of screams and shouts. Maybe I had a fever. A genital pox on any moron who sells a child a toy flute.

---

[14] This entry originally appeared in Quantum Shaman: Diary of a Nagual Woman.

On the long drive home, I was finally alone for the first time in over five days. Being a loner, I do not care much for human contact. Minds press too close. Probes attempt to penetrate. I turn to smoke.

The rental car glides easily through the desert, with Leonard Cohen's gruff voice on the CD player and massive thunderheads gathering in the west. The Nevada/California desert weaves an alien landscape. Joshua trees walk the ley lines. Jagged mountains poke bony fingers skyward. Skid marks zip the road tight to a parched earth.

Words are only tools of misunderstanding. You had to be there. But I was alone. No way to tell the tale but to trace along the edges, maybe to reveal what lies beneath. Such is the contour of the nagual, with the delicate flesh of a lover and contrastingly dangerous fangs.

Somewhere in the middle of the desert, in the middle of a long and winding road, I awakened inside Orlando. It really was that simple. Opened my eyes, looked around, had a laugh at the human condition, a bigger laugh at my mortal self going through the machinations of Life, and began to cross-ponder from what can only be called a dual point of view (Orlando and Della) this bizarre thing called Time.

Time is a mortal construct. We make it up to use as a yardstick, a reference point against the backdrop of eternity. But it isn't real in the sense we might think. Impossible to describe how it felt to be outside of time altogether. Orlando often talks about Time, but after this experience, I now realize he talks to us in much the same way an adult would talk to a 5-year old about the birds and the bees. He uses language we can understand, but the actuality of it all tends to lose a lot in the translation. Birds and bees have very little to do with human reproduction, and time has very little to do with life and death. It's just an egg in which we gestate while waiting to hatch.

While.

Waiting.

Our language itself creates Time, referencing it in countless subtle ways.

So there we were. Mortal self and eternal double driving down a winding road in the geographical center of infinity. Perhaps chance chose the space-time. Who's to say? Life seemed strange, at odds with itself in so many ways. The organic robot in the SUV behind me was flashing his lights while puffing on a cigarette and yapping animatedly on a cell phone. Funny monkey – all red-faced and angry, holding up a predictable finger while mouthing some obscenity in my direction as he zipped past on his way to his appointment with death. For kicks, I showed him my own finger in return – it was expected, after all, and I had a bigger ring that caught the sun – and with that little ritual out of the way, I turned my attention back to Orlando.

You are the final fragment of yourself, he whispered, so close to my ear I could feel the heat of him, even though logic and reason said it was only the sun pouring through the window.

"Touch me with your naked hand, touch me with your glove," Leonard Cohen murmurs in a black silk velvet voice that sends shivers down my spine, a voice that invokes the midnight even in mid-afternoon. I felt Orlando's touch. As if in a vision more visceral than stone, the thunderheads in the west trembled. A lover's caress. Lightning snaked parallel to the ground. A golden butterfly struck the windshield and entered eternity. An eagle soared over the desert, hunting. Two fine fat black ravens strolled along the side of the road, oblivious to the slipstream thrown off by a careening 18-wheeler.

"There is a crack. There is a crack in everything. That's how the light gets in." Cohen again. Wickedly perceptive old man.

I laughed, hearing it echo from here to there and back again, from the dark into the light, manifesting particle-wave duality riding itself back into the blackness, serpent eating its own tail only to turn wrongside out into some other perception of an ever-evolving reality. *You are the final fragment of yourself.*

And then I was mySelf again, just a mortal crone propelling herself down the road at dangerous speeds, cycling endlessly between one moment and the next, between here and now, drifting between the harsh terrain of Time and the snowscape of timeless infinity.

When the final fragment is integrated, Time itself will end.

"I see," said the blind man.

I *See.*

Back to the Boat

A seeker asked:
You recently talked about getting back to the boat, referencing an experience you had with Orlando wherein you said you actually inhabited his assemblage point while journeying with the mushroom ally. I'd like to know more about that. What did you see? What does it feel like to be an eternal being, an ally, an inorganic awareness?

Though there have been several instances of conjoining on a lesser level, the experience I've described about being "on the boat" was perhaps the most clear vision I have ever experienced. Not only 3-D, but 4-D, 5-D and beyond. What did I see? Ah... what did I *see*?

I stood in the doorway of my office looking toward the bookcase, and there stood Wendy with one foot up on the bed, elbow on knee, seeming to strike a pose of contemplation rather like The Thinker, or the captain of a ship pondering his course.

And suddenly the world changed, expanded, bloomed into such clarity that I can only compare it to the scene in *Contact* when Jodi Foster finds herself on that crystal clear shore of the alien world. What did I *see*? I was standing on the starboard side of an old sailing vessel, a grand pirate boat with her tattered sails lowered as we glided through still black waters in the night. The air was warm against my skin, and I *was* Orlando. No boundaries between us, no separate identities remaining. We simply *were* the totality of the Self, wholly conjoined, and I remembered when I had been on this boat, and that remembering was both in the Right Now, and also a reference to "back then" in time.

This was a memory of Orlando's life (one of many), yet it was also a memory I had given him as part of the agenda to make him whole so that he can make me whole... creator and created in their eternal dance, weaving the tapestry of Wholeness through experience. One of those experiences was this moment on this old pirate vessel somewhere in the warm Caribbean seas, a moment when the memory of "he" and "me" converged into a single point of view.

What did I *see*? I looked across the center span of the boat to see Wendy's double in the same pose she had been in when she stood with one foot propped up the bed. Except now, the body was tall and muscularly thick and undeniably male. Silver-blonde hair the color of corn silk hung to his waist, reflecting starlight, and his eyes were pinpoints of wonder and certainty, fixed at first on the horizon beyond the bow of the ship, then turning to focus on me with such an intensity that it was no different to look *at* those eyes as to look out *from* those eyes.

Without moving from where I stood, I touched him with a thought that was no less real than a physical caress. A thin sheen of sweat from the hot tropical night clung to the luminous skin. The billowy white shirt was open in the front, showing a masculine chest of hard muscle and bone, not the soft pale breasts of the feminine manifestation. A scent of foreign spices clinging to his clothes, his body. The prominent vein in his neck pulsed with life, a slow, steady beat like a pagan drum.

Water lapped against the side of the boat, and I experienced its curious caress like fingertips on my skin. But I could not take my eyes away from Wendy's Other. I have seen him in the flesh only once, and that was many years ago, rock-climbing in Joshua Tree National Park. This was undeniably the same man, just as my own reflection, had I looked, would have been the male image of Orlando as he appeared when I met him back in 1988. What did I *see*? I saw my love incarnate, and the grandeur of all existence captured in that single moment. Wholly Orlando - which is to say Wholly *mySelf* - I said to Wendy's double, "Oh, there you are." It was a given, as if we had agreed centuries in the future to meet at this appointed place and time and we had finally kept that appointment.

And in that instant, we were both in the exact same place, the exact same vision, which is to say Wendy *was* her totality, her higher self, the conjoined wholeness of herself stretching into infinity. We were *on* that boat. The timbers beneath my feet were dark wood, highly polished. Canvas sails smelling of tropical mildew. Sea air brisk with salt and siren song. The stars overhead were twinkle lights on the ceiling of the infinite, lights shining through from whatever evolution would come next, beyond even this, lighthouses on the shore of All Possibility.

We looked at one another for an eternity that night, contemplating the All, wondering aloud and telepathically to one another how it was and why it was that we truly *are* these beings on the boat, yet we are also seemingly attached to our ordinary awareness of The Sometimes Depressed Poet and The Aging Shaman Witch. We laughed about that. And our laughter spun a spidery web of energy that still echoes out there somewhere, a laughter we will one day inhabit again, infinitely and eternally.

What did I *see*? I *saw* myself. And I knew then who I truly *Am*. I saw Wendy, and had the same realization for her. And yet, I/Orlando also saw that that moment of perfection can *only* be inhabited when the warrior does the work required of her here in this ordinary world of mirrors and illusions. Wendy's Other was sad for a time that night, asking why we had to come back to this, why we couldn't just stay. Orlando knew the answer, but held it in silence for awhile. Finally, he simply said, "You have to *be* eternal before you will know how to *become* eternal. What we are experiencing right now is the Be-ing. We have to go back with this Knowledge in order to complete the Becoming, the Doing."

That's what I *saw*. And so much more that can never be wrapped in any blanket of words. And sometime not long after that experience, I wrote that poem, *Back to the Boat*.

Back to the Boat

A voice passing through the nothing whispers,
"We have to get back to the boat."
A twin-rigger she was,
with timbers creaking beneath our feet
on a sea so still
we gazed down into the midnight sky,
and the ship had become a starswimmer,
and all the stars just trinkets on your belt.
Your eyes were stolen sapphires,
your heart a pagan drum
stretched taut over the hollow
of vacant crypts and empty coffins

where our bones would be writing
sonnets of dust
had we never embarked on this treacherous trip.
"We have to get back to the boat."
Back to that place
where the rivers of reason have all run dry,
where silence has its own continuum,
and the flesh we inhabit is luminous silver,
where all of creation is our address,
all of time our identity.

Now You See It, Now You Don't

May 3, 2013

    As we were leaving Felicita Park around noon, I suddenly looked up and *saw* Orlando standing in front of a huge window in a house close to the road. The window stretches at least two stories high, is probably 10-12 feet wide, and arched at the top. He is wearing fine clothing, maybe even a tuxedo, and it is close to sunset as he looks out over the world. His feeling is one of total contentment, knowing he is immortal. He looks out over the landscape, having the thought that the world is constantly changing, yet nothing much ever really changes – a quantum contradiction that is both unnerving and simultaneously comforting.

    The main aspect of the vision is that he is utterly content within himself. He places one hand on his chest, just above the heart, and slowly slides his palm down the full length of his body, almost as if affirming the solidity of his existence. He is utterly pleased with who and what he is. The feeling was one of absolute serenity.

    This vision came out of nowhere, and has remained with me throughout the day and into the night. How I want that kind of certainty for myself – the knowledge and certainty of being eternal awareness, knowing it cannot be taken from me.

~

When this vision of Orlando occurred, I was in the car at the time. We were stopped at a traffic light and I was gazing at the house which figured prominently in the vision. This all occurred in real time and I had a clear view of the house for at least 30-45 seconds or more, while we were waiting for the light to change.

After the faire was over, we were headed into town to get some dinner, which meant going the same route as when I had the vision. Again, we were stopped at the light, and the house was simply not there. It was *nowhere* along the route, as if it never existed! I had really not thought much about the house at all - it was the vision that was relevant. It never occurred to me that I was looking at a house that does not appear to exist in our reality.

So when I realized the house isn't even *there*, I now believe some sort of dimensional overlap *must* have occurred, because there is simply no other explanation. I was looking at that house with the same degree of physical reality as I am sitting here typing on this computer. It was real. It was there in *this* reality. And it triggered the vision which has continued to haunt me for days, and which now becomes even more significant.

Whitley Strieber and others have written about wandering into neighborhoods that *appear* real and solid, yet which apparently disappear whenever they have attempted to return to them. I would put this incident in that same class, a side-trip to the unknown through a door that opens and closes of its own accord.

———

The Crystal and the Nagual[15]

> *"I am now faced with the special problem of having to explain what it is that I am doing... and I must first of all reiterate that this is not a work of fiction. What I am describing is alien to us; therefore, it seems unreal."*
> —Carlos Castaneda, *The Eagle's Gift*

> *"Does the double have corporealness? Certainly. Solidity, corporealness are memories. Therefore, like everything else we feel about the world, they are memories we accumulate, memories of the description."*
> —Carlos Castaneda, *Tales of Power*

What was it about the post office?

It was there that I first met Orlando, and there I was destined to speak with him in the corporeal world for the last time. I did not know at that time what I have come to know since. I did not know Orlando was what don Juan would have called "a nagual man". I did not know that I am "a nagual woman". And I couldn't have known then that these two beings are essentially halves of a whole - not in any petty romantic sense, but in the sense that they are mirror images of one another on the energetic plane. In shamanic terms, I was not only facing the other half of myself, but as I have since come to discover, I was also facing my own double, and it was only my ignorant naiveté that saved my life that day.

> *"No sorcerer knows where his Other is. A sorcerer has no notion that he is in two places at once. To be aware of that would be*

---

[15] Even though this appears on the Quantum Shaman website, it warrants being included in this book of the ineffable because, in so many ways, it was one of the most life-altering events of my life.

the equivalent of facing his double, and the sorcerer that finds himself face to face with himself is a dead sorcerer. That is the rule. That is the way power has set things up. No one knows why."
- Carlos Castaneda

It was late June, 1991, when Wendy and I were on our way to the Del Mar Fair. The weather was hot, the sun unnaturally bright that day, reflecting off the silvery marine layer common to southern California. We left the house around 10 a.m., but had to stop at the post office on the way. As we drove up, I saw Orlando standing in the outdoor courtyard in full black spandex - a sight that instantly sent my heart into my throat, because as much as I admired and respected this man, I was also strangely afraid of him, for history had proven that any time we met, I would find myself unsettled for days or even weeks to come. Hindsight being 20/20, it's now easy to tell that this sense of unrest was caused by the shifts in my awareness which occurred whenever we came into contact.

For those new to this type of spiritual exploration, I am not referring to the normal fluctuations in perception that are part of our everyday life as a result of fear, joy, ecstasy, or even love or hate. What I am referring to is an actual movement of the human assemblage point from its normal location (the awareness of everyday affairs) to a much more perceptive realm known in shamanic terms as heightened awareness.

In the shaman's world, heightened awareness is a highly developed state through which the individual can interact with others in a manner that facilitates the rapid learning of things which we have been programmed through Society to think of as impossible in our day to day lives. From the assemblage point of heightened awareness, we simply do not fight ourselves. In dreams, we do not question that we can fly, or communicate telepathically, or read with our eyes closed. We simply do it.

The problem is that when we return to our ordinary state of awareness, we cannot remember the majority of events which took place within heightened awareness. At first, this seemed ludicrous to me. And yet, when it was pointed out that we have literally dozens of dreams every single night, yet we might remember only fragments of one or two, it became possible to understand how time spent in heightened awareness can be entirely obliterated from our ordinary memory-perception. Indeed, it is only through a painstaking process often referred to as "remembering the other self" that we might begin to recapture those memories at all. In ordinary awareness, we simply do not possess the preceptor organs of memory for events that occurred in heightened awareness - in much the same way that we cannot see the quantum universes with the naked eye, but we can learn to see them through the use of special tools. In the case of remembering the other self, those special tools are the tools of perception.

To this day, more than two decades after the incident I am going to describe, I am still unraveling and reconnecting to events that occurred while in heightened awareness.

Recently I mentioned Castaneda to a group of seemingly enlightened individuals, and their reaction was one of lip-pursing disdain, followed by the oft-repeated statement, "My, my, but don't you know he's been debunked? Don't you know his works were proven to be fictional?" To those with a need for hard labels and neat categories, perhaps that is the perception regarding Castaneda or any other shamanic text, yet I can say from experience - from actually Doing this journey first hand - that the vast majority of concepts discussed by Castaneda have turned out not only to be accurate, but it is my opinion that in many cases, Castaneda *understated* the reality of it. To the academician in his well-lit office surrounded by the ordered structure of the university, the shaman's world is going to seem as impossible as aliens landing on the White House lawn. To those well-meaning phantom church ladies with an intense need to have the world

Make Sense, it is entirely necessary to discredit the messenger and label the message as fiction. To those who are dependent on consensual agreements, the shaman's world can only be seen as an aberration which represents a massive threat to their own comfortable status quo. And it is a perceived danger which is most often met with ridicule, disrespect, and, at times, hostility to the point of violence.

And yet, to anyone who has experienced even a glimpse of the sorcerer's world, there is no denying its validity, its reality, and its veracity.

What I did not know that day in 1991, was that Orlando was indeed a master shaman, and a great deal more. All I knew then was that there was some connection between us - not only myself, but Wendy and Ellen as well. And so when I saw him standing there at the post office that day, I was inundated with a flood of perceptions that I could not explain or even understand. Looking at him from a distance, the same words that had come to me when I first saw him repeated in my mind: *He's not human.*

And yet, despite my fear, like a moth to flame I was drawn to explore the light that he exuded. Not the bright, blinding light so often spoken of in airy-fairy new age books, but instead his luminous form was one of black light - subtle, unearthly, a dark light beneath the surface that illuminates those who are compatible with its properties, just as a black light selectively illuminates objects in a room while leaving others unchanged.

It had been six months since we'd last seen him, and as was typical with him, he did not appear the same as he had on our last meeting. We had often joked that there were two of him. In hindsight, I can only smile. To say there were two of him would be to limit what he is, what we are capable of being. He is an eternal being with an infinite number of possibilities, no longer confined by the constraints of the space-time continuum. All of us have that potential. The difference was that Orlando had already become Whole, and so there were no limitations on him. He could just as easily have appeared as a woman, a boy, or a coyote. The familiar form was for our benefit.

For reasons of her own, which she later related as simply shock at seeing him there, Wendy went inside the post office to conduct her business. Ellen (our third companion that day, and a close friend at the time) was standing off to the side, a silent observer. When I questioned her about the event years later, she could only say, "I *couldn't* go near him. This was always how it was with him, every time I saw him. I knew he would *see* through me and I wasn't ready to deal with that. It wasn't him I was afraid of. It was *myself*."

Having no such common sense, I approached him alone.

We spoke briefly – small talk, mainly - and though I could not determine why, I was inundated with the perception that he appeared nervous, even anxious. At this point, he had been in and out of our lives in a rather mysterious fashion for about three years, and had been very instrumental in changing the way we thought about life. In short, he had started us on the path, without ever taking any direct action to do so. He had given no speeches, offered no teachings, and had done nothing specific other than speak in plain, direct terms about how the world in which we live is largely an illusion, and the programs that drive the majority of human beings are little more than scripts placed on them from the moment of birth.

"We're prisoners of our own delusions," Orlando once told us. "And the worst delusion of all is that humans believe they're already free. That's what keeps people chained to their jobs, their ideas about family, society, life and the world. As long as they think they're already free, they're blind and subservient to the prison. It's a flawless trap."

At one point quite early in our association, I recall a conversation about the state of the world, and my naive comment that I hoped it wasn't too late to save the planet. He had smiled very faintly, looked me squarely in the eye, and said, "It's already too late. It always has been. You can only save yourself."

I hadn't understood his words at the time, nearly three years in the past by then. But I had been haunted by them and by the implications that there was no external salvation, his seeming Knowledge that, one day, whether in a hundred years or a hundred million years, even the planet would be laid to waste - if not by the designs and devices of humans, then certainly by some wayward comet. It was inevitable. And it didn't even seem to bother him in the least. *You can only save yourself.*

As we spoke there in the outer courtyard of the post office with these thoughts running through my head, I began to feel physically shaky, as if I couldn't stand, a sensation of dizziness, weakness in the legs, slightly blurred vision. This was not a typical reaction for me, even in the presence of someone I had pre-determined to be "not human".

With Ellen witnessing, we spoke for about five minutes, at which point Orlando simply returned to his car and drove away. Our meeting was - to my perceptions that day – unexpected, casual, but friendly. And yet, I cannot deny that there was an underlying sense of foreboding even as we stood in the shadows of the building, discussing such mundane topics as remodeling, real estate news, the growth of the small town in which we both lived. Nothing of significance. And yet, just below the surface was an entire universe of energy. It was as if two separate events were occurring at precisely the same time, yet only one was accessible to my ordinary perceptions. On the surface, just a mundane conversation that would be quickly forgotten. But at the same time, some incredible event for which neither science, religion nor mysticism has any quick answers.

It was palpable, a living force that thrummed like a heartbeat, and pounded at my senses with all the force of a hurricane. I felt it, but instinctively denied it, trying to tell myself to keep it light, don't push, and all the other yammerings of the internal dialog that are so often our undoing.

On the outside, I was entirely calm. But on the inside, all I had known about the world was coming apart in a maelstrom of energy that was destruction and creation at exactly the same moment. But like a caveman witnessing a rocket launch, I had no concept at all of *what* I was experiencing.

When he left, it all seemed rather anti-climactic. On the surface.

And yet, by the time I returned to our car, I could barely stand. My body was shaking to the extent that it was like a mild form of convulsions. And again that haunting thought which I had entertained upon first seeing him years before whispered through my mind: *He's not human.* The contact I had had with him over the three-year interim had done nothing to convince me otherwise. Now, having such an intense physical reaction left me wondering what had happened.

Wendy, Ellen and I continued on to the fairgrounds amidst a flurry of conversation, though I noticed that I was removed from it, detached, almost floating outside the car, a passive observer rather than an active participant. I cannot stress strongly enough the profundity of the physical reaction I had to this encounter, and yet it had all seemed so completely normal. Ellen confessed that she had felt something, though like myself, she had seen nothing out of the ordinary.

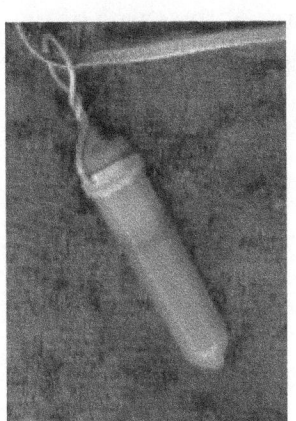

By the time we reached the fairgrounds nearly an hour later, I was feeling somewhat better, though remained in an uncharacteristic daze for the remainder of the morning. It was when I was sitting across from Wendy at lunch that she looked at me very strangely and inquired, "Did you buy a new crystal?" I had been in the habit of wearing a blue agate cut into the shape of a quartz point crystal. The problem was, instead of its usual bright turquoise blue, it was now a faded, muddy brown. Since this was a semi-transparent stone, we could see that even the deeper veins of agate had been affected, so profoundly changed that it was barely recognizable, only a few scant traces of blue.

I could only stare at the stone in disbelief, at first not making the connection to my encounter at the post office. It seemed that some incredible burst of energy had actually altered the stone down to a sub-atomic level - *while it was around my neck.* I felt the effects of this, quite obviously, but did not perceive it directly, except through the reactions in my body.

Even though I stated at the beginning that the encounter at the post office was our final encounter with Orlando on the corporeal plane, that isn't entirely accurate. The next day, as it turned out, we crossed paths with him for what would turn out to be the last time, and the unnerving thing was that he did not appear to know us in the least. This was not some act or game, but a literal blankness that has haunted us ever since, as if the spirit that had inhabited the body had simply departed. The incident occurred in a crowded restaurant, and though he was jovial and friendly with others, there was simply no thread of recognition toward any of the three of us. When I met eyes with him, I knew I was looking into the face of a stranger.

Orlando was gone.

What remained was a corporeal vessel belonging to another man, a mortal human being who clearly had no awareness of any of it.

It was only much later that Wendy and I recalled an odd statement he had made to us shortly after we first met in 1988.

"One day I'll be rude to you," he had said, standing in the driveway of his modest home, backlit by the dusky California twilight. Dark glasses had obscured his eyes that day, even though the sun had long since set. The 5 o'clock shadow gave him the appearance of a handsome pirate, an unpredictable rogue, perhaps even one of Anne Rice's vampires. No, he wasn't human. I mean that literally. And I was destined to encounter the evidence of it at the post office during our final encounter, as well as when we saw him at the restaurant the next day.

"Why would you be rude to us?" Wendy asked him.

It seemed he never heard her. "One day I'll be rude to you," he repeated. Then, with even greater emphasis, his voice softened, almost a whisper, fervent. "Don't take it personally. Don't ever take it personally."

He never explained his statement beyond that, though his words had given me chills even as he spoke them - as if he were privy to some knowledge about the future that no one else could know. And yet, when we remembered those words after his non-recognition at the restaurant, it all seemed to make as much sense as is possible in matters of sorcery.

If he was what Castaneda referred to as the Nagual man, he undoubtedly knew it, and had long since accepted his fate. He knew he would leave the world in the manner of a sorcerer, and to those unfamiliar with matters of shamanism, there can simply be no linear, rational explanation of what that means. Even as he told us in 1988 that he would one day be rude to us, it is my belief he already had knowledge of exactly where the future would lead him. And now, more than 20 years later, it is extremely clear to me that any eternal being who exists outside of time, also exists within *all* of time. Past, present and future would be equally accessible. He didn't just *seem* to know the future. He *did* know the future.

And, of course, none of this can even seem possible to a properly rational mind. It can only be reported in the same manner alien abductions or sightings of bigfoot are reported. And it will undoubtedly be ridiculed just as vehemently. The world of ordinary awareness and ordinary men simply cannot accept what it cannot categorize, what it cannot understand.

Clearly, something incredible happened during my final

conversation with Orlando, some massive rearrangement of reality on a level of which perhaps only the allies are capable. And, quite honestly, if I didn't have witnesses to this, I wouldn't have believed it myself.

That night after the fair, I took the crystal off and placed it in a medicine pouch that was always with me. Over the next few months, I would occasionally take it out to examine it or show it to friends while relating this strange tale of power, and the startling thing was that it was beginning to "heal" - the brown was slowly returning to blue. This, of course, is also supposedly impossible, or at the very least, extremely unlikely, even according to a geologist friend of mine who examined the crystal and hesitantly suggested that the crystal appeared to have been "struck by lightning."

When about 11 months had passed, I went to look at the crystal one day, and it was gone. Every other item from the medicine bag was still safely inside, yet the crystal was missing and has not been seen since.

As to what all of this means?

> *The Nagual woman came to me last... Don Juan had told me that on the left side there are no tears, that a warrior can no longer weep, and that the only expression of anguish is a shiver that comes from the very depths of the universe. The warrior's shiver is infinite. As the Nagual woman talked to me and held me, I felt that shiver.*
>
> *She put her arms around my neck and pressed her head against mine. I thought she was wringing me like a piece of cloth. I felt something coming out of my body, or out of hers into mine. My anguish was so intense and it flooded me so fast that I went berserk. I fell to the floor with the Nagual woman still embracing me. I thought, as if in a dream, that I must have gashed her forehead in our fall. Her face and mine were covered with blood. Blood had pooled in her eyes.*
>
> -Carlos Castaneda, *The Eagle's Gift*

It is my opinion that Castaneda left much unsaid, either intentionally or because the Knowledge had not yet become available to him. What he did not say is that the nagual man and the nagual woman are literally two halves of a whole, unlike any other being on Earth. And when one half leaves the world of ordinary awareness, the sense of tearing away is as much physical as emotional. It can leave evidence in the form of altered crystals... which, of course, are probably destined to disappear.

It was in November of 1994 that we began receiving communications from Orlando, and the path re-opened to consume us completely. But I have never seen him physically since that day when the crystal turned from blue to brown, when the world turned wrong-side out and everything I thought I knew about reality was obliterated completely.

It was that day when the Rule of the Nagual was set in motion in my life, and I do not believe I will see Orlando again until I have also passed beyond the Eagle to embrace the totality of myself. And, of course, when we do meet again, I have little doubt that he will be standing there in the middle of all Eternity, in the heart of Infinity, holding that crystal in his hand.

Though we are separated by an abyss, I know that only if I am successful in my bid for Freedom, my evolution of consciousness, will it be possible to reconjoin with that other half, that mysterious other Self who once walked this Earth as solid and real as any man.

Orlando has always said it's in his own best interests to teach us all he can, because only if I am successful in my evolution is the continuity of both guaranteed. There is no predestination. There are no guarantees. There is only power, intent and will. The hardest task he faces, he says, is getting us to *see* and to accept ourselves for the utterly capable and mysterious beings we truly are. As long as we fight that awareness, we remain divided by an infinite abyss of perception.

The View from the Porch

September 19, 2007

Outside my window, a raven flies toward the south, the direction of perpetual summer, the heat of the heart, the heart of the spirit. Autumn creeps closer, hard to recognize in the desert. Like a shadow not quite seen on a cloudy day. But there. Subtle. Writes its name on the wind, scratches its initials in the dust with the skittering fingers of fallen leaves.

Ever look at the tiny etchings leaves make in the sand when they are scattering toward winter? Like footprints left by time. Little hatch marks to say, *I was here and now I am gone*, when the wind comes to brush the sand smooth again, erasing even the shadow's shadow.

The nagual tells me we are no different. Brittle poplar leaves, inconsequential scratchings in the dust, tiny ants on a long trail toward a road that came from out there and leads who knows where.

The bees are dying, I'm told. The ozone has a hole in it. Global warming is a certainty. Obliteration lies just around the dark corner of encroaching time.

Should I be afraid? Funny, but I feel no fear.

I am a being who is going to die. Funny, but I know I have already embraced my totality. And so I feel no fear.

Without fear, we find the place of Silent Knowing.

And in that place, there is little to discuss. There is only the awe-filled wonder of a being who looks out toward the infinite, already knowing the infinite is the thing doing the looking.

―――

Token of Awareness

March 28, 2008

During a chat this morning, the subject came up of re-designing my website, which led to some discussion about a variety of topics. I put forth the idea that maybe moving away from some of the Toltec terminology might work better for most ordinary folk, and at some point I made the comment, "Castaneda has been dead for quite some time and many people no longer even know who he was."

Just a conversation in passing...

Upon leaving the chat room, I went outside to water some new trees we've been planting here at the house - one of my favorite not-doings - and my mind was mulling over the ideas presented in chat. In particular, I was thinking about how Carlos allegedly died in 1998, and how it seems like only a few months ago to my tonal mind. Where does the time go? What finally became of Carlos in the end. Did he make it past the eagle?

As I turned from one flowerbed to the next, my eye caught a glint of metal on the ground. About the size of one of those new golden dollars, but when I picked it up, it was nothing familiar - certainly nothing that should have been lying there in the dirt, as if dropped there just this morning.

UCLA - B (on one side of the brass coin). "Parking Token" on the other side.

A parking token from UCLA? It occurred to me that Carlos attended UCLA, but the synchronicity of timing seemed almost *too* great to be a synchronicity at all. Just plain weird.

And yet...

When I showed the little treasure to Wendy, she pointed out that it is probably old, since it seems unlikely that such a major university would still use coin-style parking tokens in this day and age of debit cards and UPC codes and the like. Maybe UCLA still uses these things - I don't know. But even if so, there's no reason it should have been found where it was, on a path I walk every day, well inside my own yard and far from the closest street. Perhaps dropped from tattered pocket of a passing spirit who was once Carlos Castaneda?

I have no real idea where it came from. But its arrival was fortuitous, to say the least - like a message from the nagual. That's what I'm choosing to believe anyway.

―――

I Died Today

August 3, 2014

I remember very little about the day itself, except that I was unusually tired. Thanks to the generosity of Wendy and our other helpers, I was able to spend most of the day in the motor home, and promised to cook hamburgers for dinner as a way of saying thanks. It was hot that day. Humid. By the time I lay down, it was somewhere around 4 pm, and though a normal nap for me might be an hour, I had no awareness at all until Wendy burst through the door at 7:30 and asked in the tone of William H. Macy in *Pleasantville*, "Where's my dinner?"

Obviously there were no hamburgers sizzling on the grill, and I had no energy to make it so. So we went out to the local Mexican restaurant in Bonney Lake instead. Friends showed up awhile later, but by that time I could barely hold my head up. Didn't feel *bad*, per se. Just tired. As if I'd run a marathon with two hungry cheetahs hot on my tail.

The rest of that evening is largely a blur. We went back to

the motor home and indulged in one of our favorite pastimes - marathoning some DVDs of *Supernatural*, curled up together on the sofa bed while the generator rattled along and what was being called the "super moon" was rising low on the horizon. After watching a couple of episodes, we turned in - me on the sofa bed, Wendy in the back of the coach.

It wasn't long before I heard myself call out to her. I couldn't breathe. My chest was moving up and down as it should, but no air was entering my lungs. Things had become surreal. I wondered at first if these unprecedented symptoms were just in my head? Was I having a panic attack or was I really on my way to Valhalla?

Taking one look at me, Wendy asked, "Do you want me to call 911?"

Normally we are both extremely conservative people where medical issues are concerned. We don't call 911 unless there is arterial spray, and only then if it can't be contained with duct tape and twine.

To my own surprise, I nodded.

Other words were exchanged, though I understood little of it as I sat on the steps of the motor home looking out at the stunning majesty of the night on which I was destined to die. Clouds shimmered over the moon, illumined from within, while Wendy ran to a friend's RV to get help. It was an incongruous paradox, or so my mind was telling me.

The ambulance came and a female paramedic began administering liquid nitro spray and a host of other medications, all of which did precisely nothing. I had the thought that this was more than enough drama. I was done. Could I please just go back to bed now?

Then I was lifted. Carried. The doors of the ambulance slammed with an odd finality and I wondered where Wendy had gone, wondered if I would ever see her, have the opportunity to say goodbye as life-long companions are meant to. I knew then that I was dying.

But then I was flying in an earthbound starship that

screamed like an angry banshee and flashed red fire all around. The paramedic was holding my hand. Seemed to be all anyone could really do.

"We're here," she said.

The world went black.

A different woman's voice leaned close to my ear and said with a matter-of-factness that was somehow reassuring, "You're having a heart attack."

And then I died.

~

I thought it rather peculiar that Orlando and his companion (actually Wendy's double, who answers to the name of "Styx") should be standing in the emergency room dressed more like characters from a Dickens novel than the timeless inorganic energy bodies they really are. Orlando was wearing a fine black tuxedo with a tall top hat, which he tipped in my direction as I sat up from my mortal remains and our gazes locked across the short distance separating us. Styx was attired much the same, though his tux was white and instead of a top hat, he was wearing a white Fedora, looking very much like a modern day gangsta. He was day to Orlando's night, yang to Orlando's yin.

I knew without knowing that they were the totality of ourselves - the perfected projection of awareness that was inorganic, eternal, and altogether immortal.

"Ah, about time you rose from the dead," Orlando said with a grin. "Just let me know when you've had enough of this hospital drama and I can end it. You won't feel a thing - at least not anything that you won't like."

Styx was looking at me the way Wendy looks at me when I'm about to do something incredibly stupid, his waist-length white-blond hair shimmering like those clouds in the light of the moon. He's always amused, always on the verge of breaking out into a storm of laughter.

"*Am* I dead?" I asked, hopping off the treatment table where a team of doctors, nurses and technicians were scrambling around my lifeless corpse, performing all manner of ritual and seeming oblivious to the fact that I was standing right next to them, waiting for the inevitable determination to be made. *'Time of death?'* The fact that no one said it only seemed to mean it was a slow night in the ER and they had nothing better to do than labor over the unmoving remains of a stranger.

So I turned my attention to Orlando and Styx instead. I found myself dressed in old jeans and a ratty yin/yang t-shirt - something I hadn't worn since the day I first met Orlando in the flesh at a post office in southern California in 1988[16] - and inhabiting a Xena-like body which I found very much to my liking. Time waved from the shadows. I was back in kenpo karate class for awhile, back in the past when Orlando was manifested in the flesh and I was young and strong and healthy and could still turn the heads of powerful men.

Styx tapped me in the center of the forehead to get my attention, but my eyes went automatically to Orlando.

Looking at him was like breathing when I had been unable to breathe before. Luminous warmth. A candle's breath. And Styx was no less mesmerizing.

Time stopped. We regarded one another the same way lovers long parted might regard one another.

"So... now what?" I asked tentatively.

The mischievous light in Orlando's eyes was almost terrifying, but at the same time dangerously alluring.

"That's up to you," he said. "You can crawl back inside your body and go on watching *Supernatural*, or you can come with us."

Much as I like *Supernatural*, it was a no-brainer. I had

---

[16] www.quantumshaman.com/html/mirror.htm To read the full story, please go to "Meeting the Mirror" on my website. The story is also in the first Quantum Shaman book, Diary of a Nagual Woman.

created Orlando to *be* the essence of my Self, the vessel of my awareness into infinity and throughout eternity. He had lived a thousand lifetimes and some, probably a lot more than that. He had spent the past 26+ years as my onboard instructor - teacher, friend, companion, lover - and there was no doubt in my mind that this was the moment every warrior both dreads longs for simultaneously.

He was the Eagle. And he was the freedom *beyond* the Eagle.

The secret, it seemed, was setting it up so that the Eagle was the Self. The ally. The betrothed. The eternal Other.

This came as a flash of understanding, but also without much ado. It was what it was. And it was good.

And yet...

Even as I was fully content with the decision to rush into his arms, seal my life and death with a kiss, and become One with The One, I thought of Wendy. I thought of my animals - Zero and Mickey and all the others. I thought of *Life*.

Seeing this, Orlando smiled darkly.

Someone in another world said something about a sinus rhythm. I reached for Orlando, but landed somewhere in the dark instead.

Orlando was prancing about in his bright, bright plumage, being the muse I created him to be. Behind him, Styx was wearing that all-white suit again. <u>You can Leave Your Hat On</u> *was playing in the background... and they were dancing again. The stuff of legends.*

~

"Looks like you're going to live."

I wasn't certain if the words were spoken by Wendy or Styx, both of whom were standing by my bedside in ICU while Orlando sat by a large window gazing out at the bright afternoon sun - atypical behavior for He Who Loves the Night.

To be honest, I didn't know whether to be happy or

disappointed. The thought crossed my mind that I had been given a second chance at life, but would I have a second chance to join with Orlando? It had been right there. At my fingertips for the taking. What might have happened if I'd simply seized the opportunity instead of hesitating?

I would not have had to skip past the eagle to be free, for I-Am the Eagle and I-Am freedom, the paradox eating its own tail.

As that thought manifested, Orlando turned his head in my direction, took off the top hat and left it on the bench as he came to stand by the bed.

He winked mischievously. "It's not too late to say yes," he said with a seductive smile. "I'll even make it quick." Then, closer to my ear, he whispered, "You'll like it. I promise."

Bastard.

I made him to be that way, of course. Every warrior gives her double the traits that will most efficiently compel her to the journey - whether solely on the level of the intellect, or all the way down to the deepest levels of a lover's midnight caress. Falling in love with the double seals the bond between mortal self and immortal Other.

For a moment or two, Wendy, Styx and Orlando morphed in and out of one another.

Time passed. Passed away.

Wendy had drifted off to sleep, leaving me alone with the two terrible imps who seemed very much to want me dead so that we could all skip off into the night and live happily ever after. *Literally*.

The thought had a certain appeal. Tied down and hooked up as I was to a breathing apparatus, a plethora of needles, and some contraption literally *stapled* to my leg, I was anything but comfortable, and *far* from convinced I was going to live, despite Wendy's reassurances to the contrary.

At one point, somewhere between life and death, I do recall showing one of the doctors my middle finger. They had taken me off sedation just enough to ask what I wanted to be done with myself. This came after I had demanded a writing tablet and pen, seeing as how I could only mumble obscenities around the breathing tube that was beginning to feel like a permanent deep-throat the likes of which would have made even Linda Lovelace gag.

What's odd about The Doctor is that I saw him as a middle-aged man, probably somewhere in the neighborhood of 55-60, with salt-and-pepper hair and a healthy physique. He introduced himself as Dr. K____, and I was lucid enough to answer the questions being put to me by the consensus.

I quickly scribbled, *Take this crap off of me NOW!*

"We can do that if it's what you really want, but you *will* die," I was informed. "You aren't strong enough to breathe on your own."

Good thing I couldn't speak.

"We can transfer you to Tacoma where they can perform a bypass," The Doctor said, as if that were the prize behind Door #1.

That was when I showed him my finger. No bypass. Watched my mother suffer through two of them, which was enough to convince me never to go in that direction.

He smiled.

"The other option is that I can go in - high-risk - and attempt to insert stents into the blocked arteries." Okay, that's door #2.

No other options were offered.

So I closed my eyes and went back to sleep.

They took my silence as a yes.

~

The whole thing reminded me of the big production number from *All That Jazz*[17], wherein the character played by Roy Scheider has had a fatal heart attack and all his loved

---

[17] Well worth renting, or buy the DVD or find somewhere to stream it. http://www.imdb.com/title/tt0078754/

ones appear in a crazy dance bit to bid him farewell.

Orlando and Styx were back, dressed more like male strippers. Well, not *like* male strippers. They *were* male strippers. Not being a choreographer, I can't really describe the moves, but suffice to say, they made the Chippendales look like amateurs by comparison.

For awhile, they simply moved to a Jamaican drum beat which was actually the chaotic rhythms of my broken heart on the monitor. They danced like lovers, coming close as if to kiss, then just as quickly breaking away in a battle of wills that had gone on for centuries.

"Come dance with us," Orlando said, crooking a finger in my direction.

And so I danced with them. Like a lover. Like a fiend. In a frenzy that was somewhere between a tango and a wild stomp through the jungle.

Wendy later told me that at some point my heart rate went over 220, and I strongly suspect it was during that frenzied, erotic quantum entanglement between the four of us. The fact that Wendy doesn't consciously remember the dance doesn't mean she didn't participate. I was *there*, after all. I *saw* her, despite what she might tell you.

In and out of time.

Time is the black hole spawned by light and gravity.

Orlando wrote those words on the air with a pen made of an eagle's feather and blood of the immortals.

I created me
  to create you
  to create me.
I created him
  to give me a reason
  to do any of it
  while balancing the multiverse
  on the tip of a pen.

Looking at Styx, then at me, he waited, pen in hand, multiverse in the offing. The affection synapsing between the two of them was palpable, a quantifiable force.

"Love is the reason," I said, recalling words he had written or spoken more times than I could remember.

I didn't just rattle it off by rote. I actually *felt* it down to the tips of my astral toes. *Love is the reason.*

Taking Styx's hand, Orlando pulled him into a tender embrace, and left the lightest of kisses on the other's lips. Then, before I understood what was happening, he came to me and kissed me in the same manner, so that I felt and tasted and simply *knew* the essence of *both* of them, and *all* of us in a single breath that was the first *real* breath I had taken in four days.

Somewhere in the real world, Wendy was standing by my side in that cold, dark hospital room. Despite the fact that she was 54, I saw her as when she was 28. And while the essence of eternity was still on my lips, I pulled her down close to me and kissed her with all the stardust and moon beams and love I possessed.

"Love is the reason," I said, though she swears I was mumbling about elves and eagles and shifting quantum realities.

The two immortals went on dancing.

Time rose from the dead.

I was going to live.

Love was the reason.

~

The only thing I might add would be a rather odd observation that took place when I went to visit Dr. K____ at his office three days after being released from the hospital.

To my surprise, the man who entered the exam room was not at all like the man I had met in the hospital - although I knew intuitively it *was* the same man. Instead of middle-aged and gray-haired, he was no more than 35, with dark hair and a more slender build. At first, I thought there must be some mistake, but Wendy clearly recognized him as the same man, and since I had absolutely no voice - I could only whisper for about four months after the breathing tube was removed - I wasn't in any position to tell the man that he had obviously sold his soul to the devil in exchange for eternal youth.

We spoke briefly that day, the typical exchange between doctor and patient, and shortly after we left his office, we began making plans for the long drive home - a 3-day excursion from Puyallup, Washington back to southern California.

In reality, of course, there was a lot more to those four days on total life support than I can even begin to talk about. It was only a full year after the heart attack that I have been able to talk about any of it at all. Not because it is too painful to remember. Not because it is too scary to remember.

But because it is too far beyond human comprehension, and entirely too mystifying to be captured in words alone.

You had to be there.

One day you will.

Until then... love is the reason.

AFTERWORD

Something I Can't Quite Name (SICQN)

Even after many years on the path, I still often find myself daunted by something I can't quite name.

Something I can't quite name... that's a good name for it. I think this SICQN may be an extension of a melancholy state of mind that isn't mundane in origin, but more along the lines of that terrible longing and loneliness I felt as an 11-year-old girl after becoming deeply hooked by Star Trek, when I stood outside that fateful night and shook my fist at the sky, and whisper-shouted, "If I can't come to you, I'll bring you to me!"

This was the most powerful statement of Intent I have ever uttered. Certainly it was a waking-up moment for me, as it is one of my only truly profound memories from childhood. Maybe it was simply the moment I went from a child to a young woman - maybe even biologically explainable in those terms - but in hindsight I now know it was the moment I went from being a phantom to being a seeker and a creator of my own reality.

This lingering sense of empty-lonely-desperate-need-to-understand-need-to-*be* I experience more often than not nowadays is not unlike what I felt as that 11 year old girl. She stood there in the Florida night looking up at the stars, somehow *knowing* it was all real in a way that no one else could understand. I felt so *very* much alone, yet I was okay in my aloneness because it was my secret world - a world that slowly began to take on a life of its own, which most adults would have said was delusional and unhealthy, yet it is probably the only thing that got me through an abusive father and the general purpose inbred morons who inhabited the small town where I grew up.

In reality, of course, it was no more delusional than anything else that answers to the name of quantum reality, but this was 1966 and few in that small town had even heard of quantum, let alone the idea of creating reality. Such things were known to be "of the devil," as evidenced by the fact that there were at least ten churches in a town with a population of less than 5,000.

So here I am, more than 50 years later, and I can look at it from opposite ends of the spectrum. I can say that everything I felt and believed back then has been validated and I now know it to be real.

On the other hand, I can also say that I am no closer to A Definitive Answer now than that 11 year old girl in the swamplands of Florida. Most people move on or move away from their so-called childhood fantasies, but that isn't possible when the "fantasy" itself is very much a *reality*.

Listen with your heart.
Hear with your spirit.
See with your third eye.

Only then will you Know.

Share in the Journey at
www.QuantumShaman.com

Orlando talks about how humans abandon their dreams and become responsible adults simply because it's easier than always swimming upstream, going against the grain, and all the other clichés we employ to talk about marching to a different drummer. But that abandonment of our dreams *is* the definition of death - because when we settle for a house in the suburbs and 2.5 nuclear children and all the trappings that go with it (PTA meetings and the country club on weekends, and the job we hate and the friends we air-kiss on each cheek at church on Sunday), that's the moment we have stopped creating reality and settled for the reality being created for us by the consensus.

Orlando's definitive statement with regard to all of this, was "The hurt is what makes you hunt a cure." And, yes, there is ultimate truth in that - I know that most seekers wouldn't be chasing this elusive reality if it didn't *hurt* so damn much. I try to remind myself that the hurt is part of the journey, perhaps the catalyst itself, the thing that keeps me forever dissatisfied with life, and at the same time in absolute *awe* of it, in absolute *awe* of who and what I *am*. And so I am forever chasing this elusive muse, this thing that gets me through the day and the night, knowing that the muse itself is of the breed that simply *cannot* be caught anymore than one can catch a shadow and hold it in the palm of their hand.

No, that is *not* depression speaking. It is *something I can't quite name*. It is *the thing itself* hiding behind a dark star, crooking a finger at us, saying, "Come on. Just a little further. I promise I'll let you catch me this time."

And of course we play the game because we *must* play the game, because we are *compelled* to play the game. But then just as we approach the shadow of the dark star, the muse is over there behind an abandoned castle at the edge of fairyland, where all the graves in the cemetery are empty, just tombstones with the names of all the mortals who became immortal somewhere along the way. And the muse says, "Ah - there you are. Sorry I couldn't wait for you, but I thought you might want to see this. And while we're at it, let's sit down for a long drink of silence and the silhouettes of your true identity. Here... just a little further... come on... this time I won't run away." And we follow because we must, even if we know by now that *catching* the muse may not be the same thing as *chasing* the muse.

"Having is not so pleasing a thing as wanting." Someone I deeply admire once said those words, and there is a truth to them that is haunting and dark and defines the journey in the same way the words "The hurt is what will make you hunt a cure" defines the journey.

Recently, coming home from Palm Springs, we were driving along the stretch of open desert that lies between Morongo Valley and the grade that goes up into Yucca Valley. Off to the south, behind the silhouette of the mountain, I saw a bright green flash that appeared to come up from the ground. It wasn't in the sky that I could determine, but was sufficiently bright that it left an after-image on my eyes. Wendy didn't see it, as she was driving, but I mentioned it to her and we were talking about another green flash we had witnessed many years ago, in our own back yard.

Even if I had shouted out, "Stop the car! Let's go investigate!" I have no doubt that we would have hiked over hill and dale to discover... *what*? It's not that I'm a cynic - quite the opposite. It's simply that I know how this always seems to end. We hike over one hill, and then there is another hill right in front of us, and we say to one another, "Well, maybe the flash was behind *that* hill, and so we keep on trekkin'. Perhaps the agenda isn't to find the source of the green flash, but to be forever chasing it. Of course, that gets more difficult as one gets older, not only from a physical perspective, but also from an emotional and mental perspective.

Most people quit chasing the muse and stop hiking over hill and dale to pursue the green flash long before they reach my age. I do feel sorry for them in many ways, but I also understand *why* they give up and go inside by their televisions and their crackling fires, and try to tell themselves "It was nothing. It was my imagination. I'm sure there's a perfectly rational explanation." It's how they deconstruct every magical part of themselves. It's how they maintain the consensual world and service The Machine, the mundane dimension. It's how they think they stay sane, when in reality turning one's back on the muse is the most criminal act of insanity I can imagine.

And yet, most people simply cannot endure this deep-longing-pain that drives the journey and manifests the muse. In my advancing age, I am convinced that Orlando and many of the other anomalies I've encountered were created by that awful ache that makes us go out and shake our fist at the sky or chase after the muse who is always on the move, always changing, yet always the same when we look in the mirror... and see that it is us out there behind the dark star, us out there in the empty cemetery, us out there.

I ask myself the question that has haunted me throughout my life. *Knowing* all these things, why am I *here*? Why am I chasing the muse instead of *being* the muse? As I said in the introduction, words I muttered to Wendy once upon a long time ago, "I don't want to be the one writing the books, I want to be the character on a grand and mysterious adventure."

Bram Stoker is dead, but *Dracula* will never die. Gene Roddenberry is dead, but *Star Trek* will live forever! Carlos Castaneda is dead, but Don Juan lives on.

What are we if *not* our dreams? *Who* are we if not the most magnificent being we can imagine? Why strive to be normal when that can only end one way, and that means to simply *end*.

Why does it have to end at all?

As long as we *accept* our limitations, we *own* those limitations, and those limitations define us absolutely. As long as the Agent Smiths on the street smile sweetly and say, "But Della, *all* things die! It's just the cycle of life," then *that* is the reality which is being sung into being because the phantoms can only sing death songs, off-key, in their mindless march toward the grave.

Occasionally in online conversations, I would test this by

posting something that would ask the question, "Do you really believe all things die? Or is it possible that there are things in this world, in this vast universe, that you simply do not know? Is it possible that immortals walk among us?" This would inevitably create an uproar, a hoopla of incredible proportions, with most of the phantoms shaking a finger and using words like "delusional" and "fantasy" and "grow up" and all the other admonitions one gives to children who may be perceived to have an overactive imagination.

Fuck the phantoms. I need my pain, as Captain Kirk once said. The hurt makes me hunt a cure.

The core of your beliefs determines the realities you see and obliterates those you choose to ignore.

The destruction of faith is the beginning of evolution.

Having is not so pleasing a thing as wanting.

This morning, the muse is hiding in a dark corner of my office, over by my old altar. It reminds me of the nights when I used to light the 13 candles and summon the shadows and call forth the ineffable with a scrap of poetry written in melted wax. It whispers, *Come back to me.* Yet it knows I never left, of course. That's just the most recent lure, the core and the heart of that *something I can't quite name.*

Come back to me.

If I followed that possibility to its logical conclusion, it is saying, "You have looked in the mirror. You know I am you. Come back to me. Come back to yourself."

Maybe that's when we catch the muse and finally open the door to that love affair with the unknown.

———

GLOSSARY

ABYSS - 1) The emptiness or the nothing, the absence of all things. Most people have never seen the abyss, while others think of it (erroneously) as the religious vision of "hell". If consciousness is existence, the abyss is oblivion. 2) The hollow emptiness inside someone who has made no attempt at their own personal evolution. The soulless void. In this definition, the abyss is the pit of despair into which people fall when they experience what is traditionally called a "loss of faith". Fortunately, it is this loss of faith and the subsequent fall into the abyss from which the journey toward evolution often begins. When faith fails or is intentionally abandoned, it is from the abyss that we begin our climb toward self-identity and self-Realization.

THE AGREEMENT (see consensual reality)

ALLY or **ALLIES** – entities or essences who may act on behalf of a seeker. Since the allies are not bound by our traditional understanding of space/time, we might have an ongoing and seemingly inexplicable interaction with an ally for years before we begin to understand that the ally is often the self, having created the illusion of separateness so as to serve as teacher and guide. Other allies, it must be stressed, are beings completely separate from the self - what sorcerers refer to as "inorganic beings". Still another definition of an ally might be the living essence of power plants – the mushroom ally, for example (psilocybin).

ASSEMBLAGE POINT (or AP) – The assemblage point is best defined as the various lenses through which we see our world. It is through learning to move the assemblage point that the seeker may begin to experience other perceptions, other "worlds". The assemblage point also moves of its accord in times of physical or emotional duress – such as the sensation of time slowing down in a moment of impending crisis, or the ability to fly such as in dreaming. A seeker learns to move/control her assemblage point, and to perceive from a unified perspective (totality) as opposed to the fragmented perspectives most humans experience as a result of the multiple roles they play without conscious awareness.

AUTHENTIC SELF – Who you are beyond all the bullshit. If you could go through an entire day without playing some sort of role (father, mother, brother, employer, employee, banker, baker, bozo, spy, just to name a few), you might catch a glimpse of the authentic self. Who are you when no one is looking and when you aren't watching yourself from the corner of your inner eye?

BELIEF SYSTEM - Any school of thought which requires belief or faith as opposed to personal experience. One example: Christianity. Another example: Atheism. Both require belief in external forces or causes, and are therefore only opposing sides of the same coin. Christianity requires faith that God exists. Atheism requires the belief that there is no God. Ultimately, neither the Christian nor the atheist can prove his beliefs, so faith of one sort or another is required in either point of view, and therefore both systems fail as vehicles to Knowledge.

BLACK IRON PRISON – the overlay; the matrix; the continuum of ordinary awareness in which mortals exist until they awaken. Term coined by Philip K. Dick with regard to his own spiritual awakening, as discussed in the book, *In Pursuit of VALIS; the Exegesis of Philip K. Dick*.

BRUJO or **BRUJA** - a sorcerer. All men or women of Knowledge may be brujos, but not all brujos are men or women of Knowledge.

BURN WITH THE FIRE FROM WITHIN – Believed by some to be the manner in which a sorcerer, warrior or Nagual leaves this earth in order to join with the infinite. Many different interpretations have been offered, but in essence I see this more as a metaphor for transcending death with absolute awareness rather than any actual dis-corporation of the physical form. What leaves the earth is the totality of awareness, the totality of Self. All aspects of individual awareness are consumed by the Intent of the warrior, so no fragments are left behind. In this manner, the warrior leaves the earth as a Whole entity.

CASTANEDA, CARLOS – Author of several books regarding Toltec traditions, including *The Teachings of Don Juan,*. From my point of view, a word of gratitude is owed to Carlos for developing what amounts to a syntax and specialized language which had proven invaluable in my own journey.

CLARITY – a warrior who has learned to *see* and maintains the assemblage point at a perpetual point of seeing may be said to have achieved clarity. Clarity may also be defined as the ability to see the world as it is, without the influence of programs or illusion.

COHESION OF IDENTITY - a state of being in which the seeker has gained a sense of self-awareness beyond all programs - i.e., the seeker knows who he or she is apart from who they are related to, or what they do for a living. There is a sense of self, an ability to touch one's own consciousness and recognize it as a whole entity rather than merely fragments associated with different roles. It is our observation that there are levels of cohesion. When the seeker has achieved cohesion, it is then possible to inhabit the Whole self (the totality of oneself) into eternity as a singularity of consciousness.

CONSENSUAL REALITY or **CONSENSUS REALITY** or **CONSENSUAL CONTINUUM** – the world of ordinary awareness, defined and shaped by what is agreed-upon by the majority of the consensus. The Real World. The societies, cultures and definitions of "reality" we take for granted, and upon which we all agree as to what is "real" and what is fantasy, what is right and what is wrong. We are indoctrinated into the consensual reality from the moment we are born, primarily through language, and yet it can be proven through simple observation that much of this indoctrination is incorrect, that what is "right" to one culture is "wrong" to another, that what is "normal" to one consensus is abhorrent to another. We live, therefore, in a world of illusions, a world of words, even a world of lies.

CONTROLLED FOLLY – The seeker who *sees* acknowledges that we live in a world of delusions and illusions, yet survival often depends on our ability to interact with that world. Controlled folly is the art of playing the game AS IF it matters, knowing all the while that all things are transient.

DEATH AS ADVISOR - it is said that the warrior lives with death as her advisor. Knowing we are beings who are going to die and face the infinite, the warrior's decisions in life are guided by the awareness. Knowing I am a being who is going to die, are my actions in *this moment* impeccable?

DEPENDENCY or **HUMAN FORM DEPENDENCY** - A dependency is anything to which the energy of the warrior is hooked. One easy to visualize example is that someone who is uncomfortable being alone with themselves could be said to have a dependency on friends, or constant input from TV., music or some other form of stimulus. Other examples, used only to illustrate the point: a constant need for approval would represent a strong dependency. Inability to break addictions such as smoking, drinking, gambling, etc., are indicative of dependencies. Only by identifying the dependencies and breaking them does the warrior free up that energy to be used for other things. It could also be loosely understood that "will" and "dependency" are mutually exclusive. As long as powerful dependencies are in command of the warrior's energy, it is virtually impossible to summon the will, because the energy required to summon the will is in use by the dependency.

DIABLERO - a sorcerer, a man of Knowledge. In some texts, "diablero" or "diablera" refers to a witch-healer as well. All wo/men of Knowledge are diableros, but not all diableros are wo/men of Knowledge.

DON JUAN MATUS - the Yaqui Indian brujo who served as mentor to Carlos Castaneda.

DOUBLE – For practical purposes, the double is the self in eternity, but can be visualized as the "vessel" into which the warrior uploads his consciousness and identity through the process of living impeccably. All warriors can develop a double, though most remain unaware of the existence of the double. The double is the energy body, developed through Dreaming to a point of extreme cohesion. The double may take on a life of its own for all intents and purposes.

DOUBLE BEING - also called "the **Nagual**". A type of human being who is simply born with two energy bodies where normally only one is present. There are countless theories, but my personal experience is that it is simply an "attribute", such as being born with blonde hair or green eyes. One cannot "become" a nagual anymore than a person with AB blood can suddenly have O blood. It has been stated that the nagual man and the nagual woman are two separate individuals, yet there are naguals who would say that the nagual man and the nagual woman are literally two halves of the *same* being. At some point in their human life, the second energy body appears to "split", and leaves the world of ordinary awareness to exist in the seventh sense, third attention, or, simply, "beyond the veil". It is the drive to reunite with the other half of one's own self that so compels the one who remains in ordinary awareness to follow the path, to respond to the lure of the other half, which serves as a beacon to Freedom. Also, and of greatest importance, it is because the half that goes into Freedom is now a being of eternity (not constrained by time and space) that it becomes possible for that half to actually instruct the mortal warrior through a variety of methods, including meditation, dreaming, gnosis, and more.

DREAMING - in the sorcerer's world, "dreaming" is an entire art form which cannot be adequately explained in a few brief words. Essentially, it is an active application of intent which enables the sorcerer to dream lucidly and navigate the dreamscape in much the same way we navigate the terrain of our ordinary awareness. Through impeccable dreaming, the double is created, and through dreaming the sorcerer begins to explore shifts of the assemblage point which enable her to assemble other worlds. Through dreaming, it becomes possible to connect the worlds of heightened awareness with the world of ordinary awareness.

DREAMING AWAKE – a level of awareness wherein the warrior enters a state of dreaming while remaining technically in a state of first attention awareness. To those who have experienced it, no explanation is necessary. To those who have not, no explanation is possible.

DUALITY - Meaning, literally, "two things simultaneously". This is *not* the same thing as dualism, which implies perception through opposites (i.e., dualism is the human propensity for perceiving black/white, good/evil, god/devil, male/female, etc) Duality implies the evolving perception which enables us to see that past and future, just for example, are no different, but only different perceptions according to our location in time. Duality can be studied in the statement, "You must *be* immortal before you will know how to *become* immortal." As long as we are locked into a linear, static perception of reality, we are prisoners of dualism.

EAGLE – according to Toltec legend, the old seers perceived an indescribable force which devours awareness at the moment of death. Though there is no literal eagle, the force itself seemed to be immense and had the shape of an enormous black eagle.

EMBRACING THE TOTALITY OF ONESELF - In shamanic terms, self-integration, beginning with the actions of the warrior in ordinary awareness and first attention, and projecting ultimately into the seventh sense, third attention, infinity. Embracing the totality of oneself would involve, among other things, the final integration of the sorcerer with her double, i.e., the conjoining of the mortal consciousness to the immortal vessel (or energy body). It could be said that the double has already embraced the totality of itself, in that it exists outside of time, i.e., not limited to the linear concept of past, present and future, but instead a ubiquitous consciousness inhabiting all of space/time simultaneously and infinitely. The double is the Wholeness of the sorcerer, but the sorcerer only becomes whole if and when that Wholeness is embraced and integrated ultimately beyond this physical/mortal life. In other words, there is no predestination. The existence of the double does not guarantee success as a warrior. The double exists by the Intent of the sorcerer until the sorcerer actually embraces and conjoins with that double into infinity.

ETERNAL BEING - An evolved consciousness that has gathered its cohesion into Wholeness, and exists ubiquitously throughout the space-time continuum and beyond. The eternal being may project (manifest) an energy body which would be indistinguishable from a corporeal body if that were the Intent, or be entirely non-corporeal, strictly as a matter of Will. See also Immortality/Immortal.

FOLLY - "In a million years, it won't make any difference." Though we go through life thinking things matter, none of them really do. Literally everything we touch in the world of ordinary awareness is folly - and yet warriors play the game as if it matters, and learn the art of stalking as a means of developing controlled folly - actions performed with the awareness that they are folly, but performed nonetheless with impeccability.

FOREIGN INSTALLATION – The program. The consensus. The agreement. The "foreign installation" is comprised of the belief systems and programs that are put onto all human beings from before they are ever conceived. We believe certain things because we are conditioned to believe them – many of these beliefs being altogether false, but when assimilated as a whole, they form what might be seen as, simply "society and culture". The foreign installation is responsible for the roles we play ("a good father should behave in such and such a manner," ... or "it is the highest honor to live your life in service to others.") Think about the things you believe, and ask yourself why you believe them. Are they true, or are you living a lie in the life of the foreign installation, doing the bidding of the hive consensus as opposed to exploring who and what you are beyond all the programming? The most important thing to know about the foreign installation is that it is US – it is upheld by the collective *agreement*. For as long as a human being exists without *awareness* of that fact, s/he is little more than an organic machine, a prisoner of beliefs that have nothing to do with reality – and, in fact, prevent her from even knowing there is a larger reality outside the agreement.

GNOSIS – an altered state of consciousness accessible through a wide variety of methods, including but not limited to simple Intent, meditation, certain mind-altering substances such as psilocybin mushrooms, tantric sex, the near-death-experience (or NDE), sensory deprivation, and many, many other methods. To me, gnosis is the most crucial tool available to the seeker, for it is through gnosis that – quite literally – the entire knowledge of the entire universe is available if one knows how to listen. What matters is that when the universe speaks, we not only listen, but apply our full Intent to the task of discovering the meaning behind the words.

HEIGHTENED AWARENESS - a state of increased perception, wherein the warrior can seemingly learn and assimilate far more rapidly and deeply than from within ordinary awareness. One of the tasks of the warrior is to "remember the other self", which consists in part of bringing into ordinary awareness the events she has experienced in this altered state of consciousness. From experience, it seems that we simply do not possess the preceptor organs of memory for events that occurred in heightened awareness, just as we cannot see the subatomic world with the naked eye. Special tools are required – in this case, the tools of perception.

HOOK WITH THE WILL – an ability of a master sorcerer or Nagual to essentially compel warriors into undertaking the journey – because any sane being who knew what they were getting into would run like hell. For that reason, it is not uncommon in Toltec practices for the nagual man or woman to intentionally hook apprentices with the energy of their own highly developed will.

IMMORTAL BEING or **IMMORTAL** - The terms "immortal" and "eternal being" are used somewhat interchangeably unless specifically noted otherwise, though by strict definition there is considerable difference. When we say "the quest for immortality begins here", it could perhaps be more accurately stated as "the quest for eternity beings here". On the evolutionary scale, it could be surmised that an eternal being has fewer limitations than an immortal still attached to organic form. Picture this: if a comet smashes the earth and the planet is reduced to rubble, the eternal being has the option of simply manifesting elsewhere, becoming entirely formless, or assembling other worlds. The physical immortal, on the other hand, might not have as many options, depending on the level of evolution of consciousness. It is speculated that there are physical immortals living among us.

INDIVIDUATION – The manifestation of the Self as a singularity of consciousness. Many paths teach unity within the all as a goal of the afterlife, whereas Individuation is the act of maintaining the unique and individual I-Am throughout eternity.

INTENT – Intent (or "<u>**unbending intent**</u>") could be loosely defined as an idea or thought-form held constantly in the quantum shaman's mind until it becomes a literal part of the shaman himself. For example, it is my intent to achieve an evolution of consciousness that will enable me to exist as a cohesive, sentient being with a single point of view continuing into eternity. The strength of that unbending intent determines the manner in which the shaman lives, which paths are taken. Intent is more than good intentions. Intent is desire in action, and works in direct cooperation with Spirit. Intent is the mother of all creation.

INTERNAL DIALOG – the automatic chatter that goes on in the human mind which is, essentially, how we keep our world intact. Internal dialog is everything from the lists we create to tell ourselves that a tree is a tree and a dog a mammal, to the inventories we run upon awakening each morning. Internal dialog, in short, is the language of the program, and one of the prerequisites to any serious spiritual journey is learning to stop that automatic self-programming so that we can hear the silence and access the deeper levels of the mind itself, including the state of silent knowing (gnosis).

KNOWLEDGE - as used throughout these documents, Knowledge shall refer to the result of direct personal experience. Example: we are taught as children that fire will burn, but until we touch a candle flame to see for ourselves, we cannot know for sure. The Quantum Shaman seeks Knowledge, never settling for faith or belief systems. The greatest Knowledge comes through gnosis.

McKENNA, TERENCE – one of the greatest forward-thinkers of this century or any other, Terrence McKenna experimented extensively with mind-altering substances and produced some of the most visionary insights into possibilities for human evolution as anyone ever has. Sadly, Terrence died in 2000, and will be greatly missed. Must-reads by Terrence include *Archaic Revival* and *True Hallucinations*.

MAGICK or **MAGIC** – as used throughout these documents, "magick" or "magic" is the force within the human organism which enables us to do, perceive and interact with things for which science has no immediate explanation. It is the force which enables a 110 pound woman to lift a 5,000 pound truck off her child in a crisis. It is the force that we recognize as "the little voice" that tells a man not to get onboard a doomed airliner. It is the ghost inside the machine, and it is altogether human. One day, science will explain "magick", and yet magick will never be fully understood, for as we grow and evolve, our "magick" grows and evolves with us – like the muse, always one step ahead so we will always be compelled to follow. Also, as used throughout these documents, magick or magic is not defined by adherence to ritual or religion. Magick is the force being *sought* through certain rituals, but magick itself is most definitely *not* ritual or religion any more than "the soul" can be found in "the church". At best, one is only a tool used in searching for the other.

MEDICINE WITCH – Sorcerer, shaman, healer, quantum teacher.

MEDITATION-WITH-INTENT - an active form of meditation as opposed to the passive silence. Meditation with intent might also be described as gnosis - the ability of the human mind to ask a question of the non-local web of all information. But more than just asking the question, meditation-with-intent enables the seeker to actually emerge with answers based in higher truth because meditation-with-intent develops the ability to listen and interact with the double. It will not happen the first time the seeker tries it, for it is a technique of learning to focus neither inward nor outward, but "non-locally" throughout space/time, in the realm of reality where past, present and future are all precisely the same, and where all information as to events, probabilities and outcomes is already stored holographically. Meditation-with-intent is tapping in to that limitless library. See also gnosis.

METANOIA – A transformative change of mind. Example: anyone can be a musician, but the truly great musicians are seized by a metanoia that makes them one with the music. In the spiritual sense, metanoia occurs when the student becomes infused with an understanding s/he did not possess previously, and which was not arrived at through linear means. Put simply: metanoia of spirit is the attainment of enlightenment.

MINDSET - a state of awareness from which we naturally assemble our idea of reality. For example, our most common mindset tells us what is possible, what is impossible, what is "real" and what is "unreal". In our waking awareness, for example, we automatically "know" we cannot fly, whereas in our dreaming mindset, we often discover that we can do many things which are "impossible" in the mindset of ordinary awareness . By changing our mindset about the parameters of reality, we can often change the limitations that prevent us from expanding and growing as individuals and as a species.

NAGUAL (pronounced "nah*wahl") - Nagual is a word with many meanings. 1) The unknowable which lies outside of human perception. The nagual is not the unknown, but the unknowable, all that cannot be discussed in any direct language, but which nonetheless exists as real. 2) The "nagual" may also refer to the leader of the warrior's party - a sorcerer, a brujo, a "man of knowledge" who is, by nature, a double being. See also **double being**.

NON-LOCAL -refers to the concept that information, consciousness and even certain types of beings may be described as ubiquitous - i.e., existing simultaneously in all places and all times. Non-local also refers to the concept that the universe - and especially consciousness itself - is a holographic construction.

NON-ORDINARY AWARENESS - altered states of consciousness such as dreaming, trance states, deep meditation, gnosis, visionary states.

ORDINARY AWARENESS - The state of consciousness which results simply by being alive and walking through life. It is in ordinary awareness that we enact our human programming. Ordinary awareness is also known as the lowest common denominator of being human. It is where and how we assemble the world and our expectations about it and ourselves.

OVERLAY - (see also **consensual reality**). Essentially, the overlay is the "play" of which we are all a part. It is the lives we live and the things we do which we mistake for "real", but which are only extensions of the human-default program. If we could see the world with the innocence of a newborn child or an alien being who knows nothing of the human paradigm, we would see the world as it really is - without all the automatic things we say, think and do because it is intrinsically programmed into us.

PHANTOM - individuals still plugged into the belief systems of the consensual reality, usually without ever questioning. Phantoms define themselves by what they do, the company they keep, the church they attend, their social status. Another mark of a phantom is that they possess an unlimited number of personalities and roles, all without the cohesion of a single, unified "*I-Am*".

PLACE OF SILENT KNOWING, THE – A "space" or openness inside the warrior where one can hear the voice of gnosis, the teacher who is often the double.

POWER SPOT - a physical location which brings an individual into balance with the earth, the non-local web of all information, and with herself. A location which enables us to focus or meditate, where we are in our most impeccable balance.

PREDATOR MIND – If it can be perceived that the consensual reality possesses a rudimentary "hive mind", it then becomes possible to *see* that this hive mind is predatory in nature, in that it invades and usurps the individual unless the individual has mastered extreme awareness. IOW, we may be "taken over" by the consensual hive, whose primary agenda is to preserve its static, status quo. Other – more extreme – definitions have been offered for the predator mind, and may in fact, have truth as well. (see also *foreign installation*)

PROGRAM - The information which we accept as truth without necessarily confirming or disproving it for ourselves as individuals. For example, we are taught, "All things die," and because this would appear to be true, most people simply accept the statement as fact rather than doing their own quest for Knowledge into the veracity or falseness of the statement itself. In reality, we cannot know for certain that "all things die."

We can only know what our perceptions reveal to us within our immediate environment. By altering our perceptions - thereby altering our automatic expectations (the program) - we learn to see that much of what we think we "know" about the world is only what we "believe". The danger of all programs is that as long as they are accepted blindly as fact, they prevent us from exploring other possibilities. If, for example, the Wright Brothers had accepted the program-du-jour which stated, "Man is not meant to fly," we would live in a vastly different world.

QUANTUM SHAMAN - a term first used by Orlando to describe one who stops at nothing in order to pursue and eventually embrace the Knowledge and abilities which will enable her to achieve a continuity of consciousness wherein we become cohesive, sentient beings with a single point of view continuing into eternity – a singularity of consciousness. The quantum shaman gathers insights, knowledge and techniques from every walk of life, from the sorcery of don Juan to the quantum experiments taking place on the cutting edge of modern science, from legends of ancient alchemy to shamanic herbalism. It is when the individual truths gleaned from these multitudinous sources assimilate to create a comprehensive "map" that we begin to understand the path toward our evolution. It is then that we are enabled through our own efforts to take control of our own destiny. This is the path of the quantum shaman.

RECAPITULATION - the process of essentially re-living through intent events in the warrior's past which have left energy hooks in the spirit. The process is described at length in the books of Castaneda; but in a nutshell, recapitulation involves disentangling those energy hooks, removing the "importance" placed on events in the past, so that warrior is freed from those hooks and as a result, enabled to go forward on his path. It is said that recapitulation frees energy trapped in the past.

REMEMBERING THE OTHER SELF – Refers not only to remembering events which may have occurred in heightened awareness, but also involves a process of beginning to "remember" the experiences of the double. It is through remembering that a cohesion of self is achieved which enables the warrior to transcend beyond the eagle and emerge as a singularity of consciousness.

RETROACTIVE ENCHANTMENT – term borrowed from Peter J. Carroll. As understood by the author, an act of sorcery in the now which may appear to have effects reaching backward in time.

RIGHT WAY TO LIVE – an intuitive awareness having nothing to do with social morality or cultural predilections. The warrior is guided by the right way to live through an intrinsic harmony with the earth, which is communicated through the inner voice of gnosis. Within every human being is the inborn knowledge that tells us right from wrong – not in any social or cultural sense, but with regard to living impeccably. Intuitively, we know that killing another human being is not "the right way to live," for example.

RULE OF THE NAGUAL – an unwritten "map" which reveals to the nagual man and woman specific truths about the path. The "rule" reveals the truth about the eagle in specific – that awareness is lost at death unless the warrior has taken measures to circumvent that inevitability. The map, therefore, speaks to *how* that inevitability may be thwarted through developing cohesion. It has been my experience that the rule itself is the same for most Naguals, but how it manifests may be very different. For example, not all Naguals form strict "warrior parties," yet they nonetheless end up guiding others to freedom in other ways. In my own life, the rule of the nagual showed me the necessity to write this book – largely for my own assimilation, and also to serve as a guide for those who find it beneficial.

SCRY or **SCRYING** - any method of divination, or, more accurately, *seeing* or gathering information or knowledge. Traditionally, to scry (or scrye) was to gaze into a crystal ball, pool of water, or other reflective object. Scrying can also refer to palm reading (as in "scrying the palm of the gods"), gnosis , or any other method of accessing knowledge and information traditionally thought to be beyond the realm of human awareness.

SECOND ATTENTION - loosely defined, second attention is the assemblage point of heightened awareness or Dreaming. It is the world the sorcerer may manifest through Intent - such as in lucid dreaming.

SEE or **SEEING** - when used in italics, "see" or "seeing" is to describe the act of viewing the world (or anything within the world) according to its true nature, without the illusions and expectations we place onto the world through our own human programs. *Seeing* is more than looking. It is the shaman's greatest asset and tool in being able to recognize the illusory nature of the consensual reality (overlay) in which we all exist, often without ever realizing it.

SELF-IMPORTANCE - Perhaps best summed up by Don Miguel Ruiz in *The Four Agreements*, under the heading, "Take nothing personally". It is self-importance that causes us to think that everything that is said or done is somehow personal to us as individuals. To get angry at the schmuck who cuts you off in traffic is self-importance. It's about *him*, not about you. The common misconception is that self-importance is arrogance, or egomaniacal behavior, and while that could be true to an extent, self-importance is more accurately an underlying defensiveness that prevents the warrior from embracing clarity and power because she is so busy defending herself, when there is nothing to defend in the first place. *It. Ain't. Personal.*

SEVENTH SENSE – a perceptual plateau comprised of a combination of the 5 ordinary senses plus the "sixth sense" of psychic awareness or, more precisely, self-awareness. Orlando coined the term "the seventh sense" to describe the "world" we are aspiring to inhabit through this evolution of consciousness – for it is a state of being every bit as real and inhabitable as our world of ordinary awareness, but accessed with a more evolved set of preceptors which could be described as consciousness itself. Some have used the term "third attention", which is somewhat interchangeable. The seventh sense is our world, but it is an expanded world

SINGULARITY OF CONSCIOUSNESS – The self made Whole, the evolution of consciousness which results in a cohesive field of awareness existing ubiquitously and non-locally, infinitely and eternally. The cohesive, fully integrated *I-Am* consisting of all components of the mortal self and the eternal double, brought together under a single assemblage point.

SORCERER – A man or woman of Knowledge; brujo or bruja. All men of knowledge may be sorcerers, but not all sorcerers are men of knowledge.

SORCERER'S WORLD - perhaps a better explanation would be "sorcerer's mindset". The sorcerer's world is the world of perception and ability available to the quantum shaman through the evolution of consciousness. Not a different world, it is *this* world, but without the limitations placed on it through our intrinsic programs and adherence to the consensual reality.

SORCERY - a system of Knowledge geared toward a direct manipulation of energy at the quantum level. Sorcery is not about frivolous parlor tricks, but is instead geared toward bringing the sorcerer into alignment with the higher self (or double) as an eternal being. The sorcerer's ultimate "trick" is to transcend death (slip past the eagle) not only retaining the awareness from this mortal life, but conjoining with the higher self so as to "**embrace the totality of oneself**" - in other words, a complete and seamless identity stretching infinitely into past and future, with the understanding that eternity is both and neither.

SPIRIT – If earth, air, fire and water are the 4 natural elements, Spirit is the 5th element of creation. The living force or anima of the universe – impersonal, not a deity or entity; the living breath of power; the cohesive element of the all.

SPONTANEOUS PARTHENOGENESIS – the act of something coming into existence out of the nothing, with no apparent cause. It is theorized by the author that the universe created itself from the void through an act of spontaneous parthenogenesis – a thought which wills itself into existence by saying I-Am.

STALKING or SELF-STALKING – the art of managing our human folly. By having a constant and keen awareness of our actions – including thoughts, beliefs and the machinations of our inner dialog – the seeker begins to throw off the chains of The Program and embrace the foundation of the authentic self.

SUPER-POSITION OF THE ASSEMBLAGE POINT – A point of awareness wherein the seeker and the Other (double) have conjoined to embrace the Totality of awareness. At this point, consciousness becomes ubiquitous, inhabiting all quantum positions simultaneously, thereby allowing for consciousness to take on certain qualities of light, at least metaphorically. Particle and wave – particle being what might be experienced should consciousness make the decision to "localize" into a specific point in time and space; wave being the non-local presentation of awareness, wherein it is a ubiquitous field spanning all of space/time simultaneously.

TALES OF POWER - sorcery stories, usually incredible and often unbelievable by their very nature. To the ordinary man, these tales would automatically be deemed to be fiction, lies, or delusions. Only to fellow sorcerers are they descriptions of acts of power, describing very real events.

TENANT, THE – a being referenced in the books of Carlos Castaneda, seemingly a self-created immortal in corporeal manifestation. Also called "the death defier" because s/he has seemingly lived hundreds of years.

TEFLON WARRIOR – Referring to the practice of recapitulation. Many (most) believe that recapitulation involves lengthy processes of reliving past experiences as a means to recapture energy still stuck in the past. That's the abridged version. If you want to know more about recapitulation, try Googling "Carlos Castaneda and recapitulation". I myself am an advocate of becoming a teflon warrior – an advanced technique which encourages detachment in the Now, so that one's energy doesn't become fixated on transient events. Note: ALL events are transient. Shit don't stick to a teflon warrior. It's that simple.

THIRD ATTENTION – the state of freedom beyond the eagle, when the warrior has achieved the state of Wholeness. The state of the ubiquitous, non-local singularity of awareness.

TONAL – the world of matter and men. Anything that can be discussed or known is within the tonal. The nagual is the unknowable, by contrast.

TRANSCENDENCE - wherein the seeker sheds his/her body through the process known as Death. In theory, those who transcend become pure energy, existing at a level of consciousness/awareness without any physical form whatsoever. Some consider this the highest form of transformation, others (myself included) consider it a midrange accomplishment.

TRANSFORMATION – In some instances, spiritual evolution may be achieved through the process of transformation, essentially having the full awareness of the Other inside one's physical body. While this is a possibility, this author believes that the sheer amount of data contained in the quantum nature of the Other would be sufficient to "overwhelm" the biological components and perhaps result in a form of alternating genius and madness.

TRANSMOGRIFICATION – The process whereby an individual may depart the physical body and inhabit the Other, without the actuality of dying. While considered theoretical, it is believed that many beings throughout history have transmogrified. The most common myth is that of Jesus. Another would be the vampire Lestat. Transmogrification is the migration of awareness from a physical/organic body into a state of pure energy – i.e., the awakening of awareness inside the Other. Transmogrification is the art of transcendence and transformation combined - in that one's awareness is no longer attached to corporeal form, but a *seemingly* corporeal body CAN be projected and inhabited.

TULPA – the seemingly physical manifestation of a thoughtform, usually transient and without individual volition. It is believed by some (including the author) that these thoughtforms *can* become sentient and take on a life of their own if nurtured. When that occurs, it might be observed that the tulpa has become the precursor/paradigm of one's double or Other.

TWO PART MIGRATION OF THE SOUL – the process wherein the mortal self creates the double through dreaming, at which point the double begins teaching the mortal self the path of evolution of consciousness. The mortal self *appears* to create the double first, and so the double exists as an eternal being, a construct of will and intent. That "immortal" then teaches the mortal self *how* to evolve, so that when the process is complete, the mortal self reconjoins with the immortal double beyond the eagle's reach.

WARRIOR – a seeker of knowledge who has made the commitment to the path of her heart. The warrior is the traveler on the journey toward becoming a woman of Knowledge.

WHOLE SELF – The integrated totality of the mortal self and the eternal double as it comes together in a single assemblage point of cohesion beyond the eagle. From the AP of the Whole Self, all memory of all fragments of the Self come into alignment. See also – **singularity of consciousness.**

WILL - Will is the force which manifests want or need into reality. Will differs from intent. A simple analogy: intent is a true and genuine plan to visit the Grand Canyon. Will is the force that puts you behind the wheel of the car and drives. Will could also be described as the force which causes the intent behind our magic to actually begin to manifest. It is the secret ingredient of sorcery, elusive as the wind and just as impossible to define.

> Love is a quantifiable force.
>
> When you understand that, you will have the power to finally be free.
>
> Free Your Mind at Quantum Shaman.com

About the Author...

Della Van Hise is a native of Florida, transplanted to California at the age of 21, who has subsequently sunk her roots into the high desert near Joshua Tree National Park. She has not personally seen any aliens since around 1992, but there is rumored to be a secret UFO base underneath her house.

Della's writing started around age 11, on an old Smith Corona typewriter. No, not an electric one. A real antique, made of metal and heavier than a wet coffin. Her first professional novel was *Killing Time* - the controversial *Star Trek* book which was recalled and re-edited in 1984. None of the rumors were true, of course. It was just a *Star Trek* book - a good enough work that the "reboot" movie borrowed heavily from the plot and structure. No kidding.

Della has written extensively in the non-fiction genre, with titles such *as Quantum Shaman: Diary of a Nagual Woman* and *Scrawls On the Walls of the Soul*. *Quantum Shaman* focuses heavily on the author's metaphysical explorations and experiences, while *Scrawls* is a continuation of those journeys many years later. If you enjoyed the works of Carlos Castaneda or Don Miguel Ruiz, you'll enjoy the non-fiction works of Della Van Hise.

In addition, Della has written professionally for *Tomorrow Magazine* and other prominent science fiction publications. Her fiction works include *Sons of Neverland* (an award-winning vampire novel); *Coyote* (a young adult thriller); and many other novels, short stories & poetry collections.

All of the titles mentioned here are available through Amazon, or through Eye Scry Publications.

www.EyeScryPublications.com
www.QuantumShaman.com

<u>Questions Along the Way</u>
**Conversations With
a Quantum Shaman**
<u>Della Van Hise</u>

Anyone on a journey of personal growth and enlightenment is sure to come face to face with difficult questions that will keep them awake at night and may even plunge them into the dark night of the soul. In *Questions Along the Way*, Quantum Shaman Della Van Hise talks frankly with seekers on the path of heart and opens wide the door to a new understanding that lies beyond the false belief systems and cultural programming all of us must confront when emerging from the dark into the light.

Who am I?
Where am I going?
Is there a God?
Are our lives predestined?
Why am I here?
Who *am* I?

The first and the last question are always the same. And somewhere in between lies the proving ground which we refer to with a simple 4-letter word known as 'Life.' Perhaps for many people these gnawing and persistent questions are nothing more than passing dalliances. But to anyone on a serious path of spiritual evolution and personal growth, these questions form the basis for "the path with heart" - a term used by anthropologist Carlos Castaneda to describe the process of going from an ordinary human being to becoming a man or woman of Knowledge.

www.quantumshaman.com

http://www.amazon.com/Questions-Along-Way-Conversations-Quantum-ebook/dp/B01A4MPLI4/ref=asap_bc?ie=UTF8

Quantum Shaman: Diary of a Nagual Woman
Della Van Hise

"Diary of a Nagual Woman brings a quantum understanding to what has traditionally been believed to be a mystical path alone. This book picks up where Carlos Castaneda left off to take us on a roller coaster ride of our own forgotten power..."
- Michael Grove, Reviewer

When I asked how Orlando had known I would come to this remote location, and how he himself had gotten there – since there were no other cars in the tiny parking lot – he only smiled a little, stretched out his long legs, and slouched down on that cold metal bench to stare up at the stars.

"You're predictable," he said as if I should have already known. "I'm here because this is where you come when you're mad at the world."

I attempted to engage him in a conversation of just exactly how he knew I was mad at the world, since I'd had no direct contact with him in quite some time, nothing to give him any hint of what was going on in my everyday life. But even as I began spelling all of that out to him, he brushed my words aside with an easy gesture.

"Do you want to talk or do you want to waste time looking for logical explanations for every magical thing that ever happens?" he asked. "That's what's wrong with the world, you know. Instead of embracing the mysteries and trying to determine how they might open a crack in an otherwise humdrum, pre-programmed existence, people waste their entire lives explaining it all away, attaching labels to it, filing and categorizing it until it loses any meaning."

He had a point. And I'd already been inundated with enough mysteries to know that some things simply had no explanation humans could understand. *'Magic is only science not yet understood'.* Words Orlando had written more than a year before rattled through my mind up there in the middle of the night, in the middle of nowhere, looking down on a distant world that seemed far more unreal to me at that moment than the world he had been trying to teach me to *see*.

He was there – whether physically or in some spirit-form is ultimately of no importance, for in the sorcerer's world there is no difference between body and spirit, and in any world, perception is reality.

www.quantumshaman.com
www.eyescrypublications.com

Scrawls on the Walls of the Soul
Della Van Hise

The long-awaited follow-up to Quantum Shaman: Diary of a Nagual Woman. Stands alone, or order together!

"If you've ever felt like a stranger in a strange land, this book is your road map to survival in the spiritual wilderness!" (Michael Grove)

~

It was May of 2000 when my mentor threw me out of the quantum cosmic classroom and said, "I've taught you everything I can. Now it's time to take that knowledge and slam it up against the walls of the real world. If it remains intact and survives the brutality to which it will be subjected, you will get a gold star next to your name and be allowed to proceed to the next level." No mention was made of what this next level might be, or if, indeed, it truly existed.

Go ahead – try to explain this all-consuming path to your friends and relatives. They will smile politely, squirm uncomfortably, and eventually they will stop returning your phone calls and look the other way when they see you coming. And who can blame them? They live in the real world with their office jobs and nuclear families and a host of mindless sitcoms waiting on the propaganda box at the end of their busy day. In direct contrast, it could be observed that anyone who has dedicated themselves to the pursuit of forbidden knowledge really doesn't live in that world at all. Not for lack of wanting, perhaps, but because the real world is quickly seen to be little more than a series of programs and illusions – not unlike The Matrix. And not surprisingly, the people who populate that world may begin to take on a peculiar zombie-like quality.

You find yourself alone in a world of jesters, jokers and jackasses. Now what?

FROM THE AUTHOR
www.quantumshaman.com

ON AMAZON
http://www.amazon.com/Scrawls-Walls-Soul-Della-Hise-ebook/dp/B008CUKH6C/

The Effect of Moonlight on Tombstones

(A Dark Little Collection of Poetry Gleaned From the Gnosis of Vampires and Songs of the Muse)

Moments Frozen In Time

Poetry has never been something I consciously set out to write. Instead, it is something that comes or not, entirely at the whim of whatever it is that writers call "the muse." Over the years, I have come to think of my own poetry as a form of shorthand - an attempt to capture a moment frozen in time. A wayward leaf caught in mid-fall. A glimpse of a shadow cast by nothing at all. The effect of moonlight on tombstones.

Though I write primarily novels and nonfiction, I do find myself pleasantly haunted by what my mentor once referred to as "the gnosis of shadows." As another friend once said, "Poetry is the streaming download from the broken heart of the universe."

The poems in this anthology represent approximately two decades of those streaming downloads, most of which were scribbled hastily and in bad penmanship into cloth journals. If I have been at all successful in capturing some of those moments frozen in time, perhaps a line or two will resonate with you, hopefully bringing a smile to your face or a chill to your spine.

Candles keep journals
of time's passing
in empty books of matches.

The cemetery lies empty,
pallid headstones only coloring books
for the idle hands of time.

ON AMAZON
http://www.amazon.com/Della-Van-Hise/e/B003ZOK75G/ref=dp_byline_cont_book_1

FROM THE AUTHOR
http://www.eyescrypublications.com/html/moonlight_tombstones.htm

*When Terrans came to sail dark seas,
And see what stars might be...
Heaven moved with no forwarding address,
And left this void to me.*
(Children's song from Lazali)

———————

A literary science fiction novel told in the voice of an empath, *No Forwarding Address* explores the lures and the dangers of love, the tragedies and triumphs stirring in the human heart.

When Crystal and Raine first meet, it is 50 years after The Great War on Earth. They are hesitant to trust, afraid to love. But even if they are able to overcome these seemingly insurmountable obstacles, is even love enough?

When a man has the stars in his eyes, legend says he must serve them above all others.

———————

I knew then that it wasn't love and hate who were mirror twins. The final irony was that <u>grief</u> would always turn out to be the paradoxical antithesis and simultaneous manifestation of whatever it is that humans call love.

Crystal remained silent and walked a few steps away from Raine – further down the shoreline, until she stood under the wing of one fallen Phantom. She thought of the ship she had seen from the balcony of our home, and though it had long since disappeared over the dark and treacherous abyss of the ocean, its image lingered clearly in her thoughts. On that ship was a man, she thought. A terribly lonely man who made no great difference to the flow of time or the memory of the galaxy. A man who, like Raine, was compelled to keep moving and look only ahead and never behind. A man who could not afford the luxury of waving goodbye to friends on shore.

At last, she turned toward her beloved and watched him watching the darkness. He stood only a few feet away, yet the images in my mind said he might as well have been a million light years off in the void. He was lost to her in that instant out-of-time, just as lost and impossible to find as the light from that ship which had vanished over the horizon...

www.eyescrypublications.com
http://www.amazon.com/Forwarding-Address-Della-Van-Hise-ebook/dp/B00PEOSKJ0/

COYOTE
Della Van Hise

A Novel of Love, Honor and Personal Sacrifice...

When River Willows is accused of a murder she didn't commit, her life takes a turn toward the sanctuary of a world existing at right-angles to our own. Combining the mysticism of martial arts and the romantic conflict of a young woman torn between two powerful men, COYOTE takes the reader on an epic journey of dangerous secrets, military cover-ups, and the infinite heart of the peaceful warrior.

"So who's Coyote?" I asked, trying to ignore the effect he was having on me. "You?"

Steale laughed easily, though it did little to hide the torment behind that mask of indifference he wore so well.

"Coyote's a scavenger, Jack of all trades. The Native Americans call him the trickster - the one who brought chaos down on the world." He shrugged as if altogether unconcerned. "Original sin."

"Is that what you are?" I asked, keeping it light despite the growing knot my stomach. "Original sin?"

He kept his profile to me, eyes straight ahead as he drove. "Sure you want to know?"

I couldn't help wondering if I had cornered the coyote, or if the clever trickster had cornered me.

By the author of **KILLING TIME** – without a doubt the most controversial **STAR TREK** novel ever published!

From the author
www.eyescrypublications.com

On Amazon
http://www.amazon.com/Coyote-Della-Van-Hise/dp/0976689782/

Turn Left at November
Wendy Rathbone

Visit realms of diamond rain, dust-folk lands and valleys of curses and shame. Reside in the burning moonships of dream, the silt of stars, the asphyxiation of the waking day. Meet the golden android who houses your soul. Journey through tatters of stardust down roads of sorrow. Find hope in planets of candles and crazy-eyed mermen. There you will meet November in these rich and evocative poems by Wendy Rathbone.

Unmaking Autumn
Out at the excavation site
where they are taking apart autumn
leaf by fabled leaf
the searchlights try to catch us
putting the eyes back into the pumpkins
the moon back in the witch-shaped sky
We steal blood kisses
behind the naked apple orchards

Winter's Shelf
hidden pathways to the moon
the north's blue breath
star-rise
amethyst dusks
winter wind bottled
and sold here

ON AMAZON
http://www.amazon.com/Turn-Left-at-November-Poems/dp/1942415087/ref=asap_bc?ie=UTF8
FROM THE AUTHOR
http://www.eyescrypublications.com/html/november.htm

TEACHINGS OF THE IMMORTALS
Mikal Nyght

So... You Want To Live Forever?

The teachings are presented as brief vignettes in no particular order of importance. This is not a book you read from start to finish in a single night. It is a grimoire of self-creation, intended to be contemplated slowly so as to be assimilated wholly. Pick it up and turn to a page at random. Where your eyes come to rest on the page is your lesson for the day.

The teachings are seduction as much as instruction. This is the Way of The Dark Evolution.

The Ruby Slippers

The danger of the consensual continuum is that its natural gravity exists at the lowest common denominator of human experience, and because of this it will automatically make you forget those elusive truths you've fought to learn, and before you know it you're lost in petty dramas again, sinking into the mire of old familiar scripts.

The only way to overcome this is to be continually cavorting with worlds and events beyond human experience, journeying into the unknown so that it can become known, expanding knowledge and awareness to become more than you were, bringing back from the Dreaming those secrets which will teach you how to use the ruby slippers to transport yourself over the rainbow to the vampyre wizard's secret lair.

Perception

This is the nature of reality: to be precisely what perception dictates, as solid and whole as your interpretation of it, or as changeable and eternal as you permit it to be.

It wasn't knowledge god tried to keep from Man, you see. It was perception, for perception alone has the power to destroy god and obliterate comfortable consensual realities to create unending immortality.

Take the apple, my embryonic children. Nibble its red red flesh. Open your vampyre eyes so you may finally begin to See.

www.immortalis-animus.com

Eye Scry Publications
A Visionary Publishing Company
www.eyescrypublications.com

www.ingramcontent.com/pod-product-compliance
Lightning Source LLC
LaVergne TN
LVHW041332080426
835512LV00006B/411